CEO in Stilettos

Unleash Your Leadership Power and
Step into Your Greatness

By Garri Davis

978-1-948777-18-6

ENDORSEMENTS

"There isn't another book on the market that captures the plight of the female entrepreneur and provides proven leadership strategies to help strengthen their organizations, navigate the world of business and learn how to do it with class and professionalism. Garri has taken the concept of a stiletto and used it to create a roadmap for business success. This is a must-read for all female entrepreneurs interested in transforming their organization and excelling in their business."

Lisa Nichols
CEO, Motivating The Masses

"CEO in Stilettos is a remarkable analogy between the different physical parts of stilettos and the interpretation of roles they play. Garri Davis highlights the importance of effective leadership and how leaders should engage and listen. Other memorable lessons in this book emphasize the value of relationships, respect and connection of the staff and active review of the overall vision of the company. Fantastic Read!"

Dr. Ali Griffith
www.draligriffith.com
CEO & Small Business Coach

"Garri gives us a savvy presentation of professional advice designed specifically for women. Her words pave the way for any entrepreneur or CEO to move toward success."

Chara Fisher Jackson
Executive Director and CEO of Cincinnati Preschool Promise

"As a business owner for over 20 years, it is inspiring to work, learn, and grow with so many people. Garri's book, CEO in Stilettos, is a well of information that is overflowing!! From how to treat your employees and giving them opportunities to advance, to creating the ideal work environment. The list goes on and on. This is a must-read for anyone in management or pursuing a leadership role."

Amy Ostigny
Owner of The Amy Ostigny Company

"Garri Davis has written an inspiring book that provides answers to many of the questions that professional women may have. Her book is an easy ready and provides support to women on all levels."

Ryan Caldwell
Waverly's Hope Child Care LLC, Owner
Waverly's Consultant LLC, Founder and CEO

"Tools for success, which we often neglect. Garri nails it.
As a parallelpreneur, who is always on the go, this is a quick reference guide that stays on my desk."

Cassandra Edghill
CEO-Sandi's Edge, Operations Executive at MTA
Bridges and Tunnels

DEDICATION

This book is dedicated to my father W. Maurice Davis (March 3, 1939–June 23, 2018). Throughout his life, he encouraged me to be a leader. He instilled in me the values of integrity, kindness, and forgiveness. He raised me to be strong, to always stand up for what is right, to be fearless and not shrink away from challenges. There is nothing that could ever take the place of the love of a father. I hope I have made him proud. I will forever be a daddy's girl.

TABLE OF CONTENTS

ACKNOWLEDGMENTS

Thank you to my supportive family and friends. You all have been the wind beneath my wings, and I would not have been able to do anything without you.

Dakari Jones, thank you for being supportive, for your love and hugs, and for celebrating all of my accomplishments. For helping me to laugh in times of stress and for being a great listener whenever I needed it. And thank you for being ready for an impromptu Beyoncé concert at any time.

Elijah Jones, thank you for being my voice of reason and my shoulder to lean on and cry on. You amaze me. Your growth, strength, integrity, and persistence define your character. And you are really funny sometimes. I appreciate your calmness in the midst of my storms and your ability to pull me out of them.

Daelyn Jones, your sweet kisses always put a smile on my face. The day you were born was one of the best days of my life. Thank you for being so smart, charming, lovable, and cuddly, and for all of the great conversations and our fun shopping trips.

Haniya Ramsey, thank you for being in charge of the kisses.

Sondra Davis, thank you for your continued love and support throughout my lifetime.

Lamont Butts, thank you for all of your love, support, and encouragement. I couldn't do it without you.

My Friend, Claudia Clayton, I miss you so much. I feel you around me often. Thank you for keeping me grounded, protecting me, motivating me, and believing in me. Thank you for keeping my secrets.

Thank you to Lisa Nichols, who provided a safe place for me to find me. You have been an amazing influence on my life and my growth. I love you, and I appreciate all that you have taught me.

Thank you to my bonus children, Juwaun Tye and Bria Stone, you keep me happy and smiling.

INTRODUCTION

The purpose of this book is to provide female entrepreneurs and leaders with the tools necessary to build confidence and success. To help level the playing field and shatter the glass ceiling. To allow women to walk boldly into the break room or the boardroom with self-assurance and conviction. To create a sense of empowerment, influence, and greater self-worth.

Whether you are brand-new to the entrepreneurial world and are just now stepping into a leadership position, or you are quite familiar with this way of life, you have undoubtedly encountered hurdles along the way. And I'm here to help you to step over these hurdles in stilettos.

Being an entrepreneur comes with its own set of challenges, and being a female entrepreneur can often be even more trying. From finding a happy work-life balance, exercising good time management skills, hiring and keeping talented staff members, and trying to stand out among the competition, it's no small feat.

The inspiration for this book is my own experience in the entrepreneurial world. I forged my own path through this challenging landscape, and now I hope to walk side by side with you and be a resource to help you do the same.

As a single parent, I graduated with a master's degree and a 3.9 GPA. I completed this degree while working a full-time job. My dream had always been to be the chief executive officer of someone else's company. I was never confident that I would be able to be the CEO of my own organization. After graduation, I made it my mission to impress anybody whose path I crossed. I worked smart, I worked hard, and I worked long hours. I networked with my superiors whenever possible. I attempted to get promoted within several companies, but I was unable to do so, and it always came down to two reasons.

The first reason was that I lacked communication skills. This was extremely hard for me to accept because I worked directly with customers and spoke with them daily. They were able to comprehend everything we discussed and take action per my directives. Furthermore, I was usually the person sought out in my department to work on different projects, to work with other leaders in the organization, and see the projects through to completion.

The second reason I was struggling to advance my career was my need for professional development, or at least that is what I was told. This was shocking to me because I had been working ever since I was a teenager, and I'd sought out professional development several times a year on top of having three college degrees and four financial brokerage licenses.

Working so hard to impress others and be recognized proved to be almost detrimental. One day at work, I began having shortness of breath. I was on my way to a professional development training, and upon arrival, I had to immediately sit down because I was feeling suffocated and finding it hard to breathe. As I sat through the training, it was clear that my heart was not beating properly. I thought I was about to die, but I did not want to bring unwanted attention to myself. For some crazy reason, my thoughts turned towards worrying about how this would affect my career, especially if this thing wasn't life-threatening, I knew that I would have to return back to work. I was not feeling better and decided that I had no choice but to quietly exit the class and go to the hospital. I was diagnosed with arrhythmia. The doctor informed me that this was caused by stress and anxiety and sent me home with strict instructions not to return to work for a week. I needed rest.

I slept and rested and rested and slept. And at some point, during that week, it hit me that I was not happy at work. I was unfulfilled, unappreciated, overworked, and underpaid. Every day, I was looking for a stranger to see me, to see potential in me, to believe in me, to see value in me. I wanted someone to recognize me for my contributions, offer me a promotion, and give me the raise I needed. But the reality was, I was just a worker bee. I was trading time for money. I was invisible.

I faced the hard truths. How could I influence someone who couldn't even see me? And what could I have done that I hadn't already tried to do to impress my employer? It was suddenly crystal clear that I would need to make some quick and immediate changes. I could either find another employer or become my own boss. I chose the latter. It was an easy decision. If I was going to work to the point of exhaustion and end up in the hospital with an irregular heartbeat, I wanted to do it for myself for my own business, not someone else's.

I wanted to do something impactful that would allow me to contribute to humanity and make a difference in this world. I'd always wanted to work with children, and so I decided to start my own childcare center. I spent the next few months gathering information, studying childcare rules, and seeking out locations while still going to work every day and being a full-time mom. The universe must have been in alignment in the Spring of 2011, because that's when I was let go from my job, and the door opened for me to become an entrepreneur. I emptied the $10,000 from my 401(k) and started the process of becoming the proud owner and CEO of my own organization.

Since then, I have grown my childcare business from one student to serving over 150 children every day. All the while, I've been helping women just like you and me start, scale, and grow their businesses. But I didn't get to this point without a long, uphill climb.

I started my entrepreneurial journey as a single parent with two children while still working in a corporate environment. Although I was being paid a living wage, I still found it difficult to provide the necessities for my family. Money was tight, and there were times I couldn't afford to feed my children anything other than pancakes for breakfast *and* dinner. At dinnertime, I would often light a candle. My children thought it was a special occasion to eat dinner by candlelight when, in reality, I simply was trying to save money on my utility bill.

It didn't seem like my situation could get much worse—until I was fired from my job with no prospects for other employment. It was then that I realized it was time to invest in my success. With all the knowledge and expertise I'd gained over the years, I chose to finally believe I was equipped to step into the entrepreneurial arena. It was my time to shine. From that day forward, I pressed on to ultimately create my own empire and become a Lead(H)er CEO!

It wasn't easy. I faced many disappointments, trials, and even failures. During those times, what I really needed was support, guidance, and good advice. That's what I want to provide for you. On the following pages, I'll share helpful tips and tools that will save you time, money, and embarrassment and will allow you to become successful and enjoy all aspects of being an entrepreneur. Believe me—these are things I wish I knew when I started out.

When we come together, support and believe in one another, and invest in each other, a sense of camaraderie forms, and what results is a tribe of successful individuals ready to conquer the world. Leaning on one another makes us stronger every day, and with that kind of support, success is inevitable.

So lean on me, and let's get started!

POWER OF THE STILETTO

Historically, the term stiletto originates from the Italian and Greek languages. In the 15th Century, a stiletto was any blade or a knife featuring a long slender needle-like pointed tip and triangular cross-section and was used as a fighting knife, a dagger, a weapon.

Today stilettos are influential and represent a fashion symbol of modern sexuality. Stilettos are known to increase attractiveness and make women feel more beautiful. Even studies have shown that women view the stiletto as an essential item for increasing self-esteem and self-confidence.

There are superpowers in the wearing heels. Influential women wear heels to emphasize power and femininity. Women are more convincingly strong and poised and walk with a commanding stride. The wearing of stilettos makes women feel ambitious, powerful, and unstoppable.

This book is a guide to provide you with a secret weapon to use as you build your business to become better informed, increase preparedness and become more assertive to not only stand toe to toe with your competitors but to step right over them into your greatness! So ladies understand that, from now on, people will not be responding to your stilettos but the confidence that you exude while wearing them.

Anatomy of a Stiletto

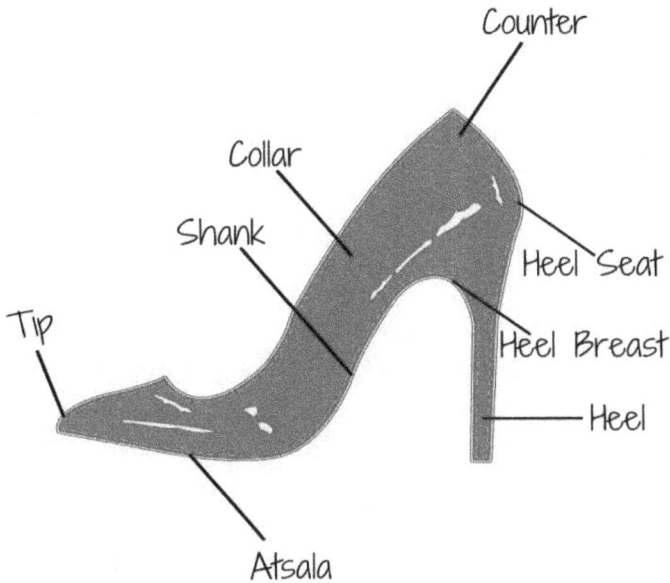

Counter	Transformational Culture
	Stiff piece maintains shape (of organization)
Tip	Employee Experience
	Must fit comfortably with room for toes to spread out. Employees must feel comfortable and like they fit into organization
Collar	Systems
	Stitching forms rim of shoe. Systems help hold organization together and running smoothly

Shank	Navigating the Glass Cliff Bridge between heel and foot. Bridge to advancement in organization
Atsala	Self Care – For traction to keep from slipping. Must take care of self to maintain in the workplace
Heel	Professionalism – Quality of the heel determines its durability and ability to hold weight. Must be maintained in the organization for credibility, advancement opportunities, etc.

TRANSFORMATIONAL CULTURE

While the primary goal of any business is making a profit, a close second should be striving to create a work culture comprised of purpose-driven leaders and employees. When such an environment is nurtured, the profit margins grow. For any company, it's advantageous to have people who are dedicated, talented, and motivated to achieve a common goal. This goes a long way in generating positivity and prosperity.

If you take any stiletto from your closet and disassemble it, it's no longer a stiletto, right? You can't wear it, let alone walk around in it. These random shoe parts don't serve a purpose on their own. Attaching these parts intentionally and systematically, however, will result in a gorgeous pair of stilettos you can feel confident in—as long as the parts are assembled well and correctly. Putting together an efficient and exemplary organization is much like the assembly of a stiletto.

The counter of a stiletto is arguably one of the most important parts. It is the stiff material at the heel of the shoe and holds the foot firmly in place. The counter is stiffer than any other part of the shoe and helps maintain the shape of the shoe. Your leadership and intentional decision-making will help maintain the shape of your organization.

Transformational culture is about shifting your company's focus from making a profit as being the only sign of success to the people responsible for making that profit. The people who make up your organization are the backbone of your company. It's not as simple as finding a handful of satisfactory employees. The goal is to find passionate, creative, motivated individuals, and put them to work doing what they do best. There's a spot for everyone, and not every person can do every job. A people-focused workplace culture begins with an effective leader.

Some people ask if leaders are born or if leaders are created. I'd venture to say both. Some women are natural-born leaders. The qualities needed to take charge are innately ingrained within them. Think Oprah Winfrey or Sandra Yancey—both amazing entrepreneurs. Unlike them, I was not born a leader. I had to work very hard to cultivate my leadership skills. In college, I took additional professional development and leadership courses. I follow successful people on social media for inspiration and motivation, and I study and emulate other successful business owners, speakers, and leaders.

But, at the end of the day, a leader is a leader, whether they are born or created. Some things they have in common—drive and determination, the desire to excel and succeed. The key to being a great leader is having the initiative, the fortitude, the proficiency, and the desire to be a changemaker. It's not the number of times you will fall down, but the number of times you get up that will define you.

There was a time when my organization was filled with gossip, negativity, high turnover, and dissension. At that time, I found it hard to stand tall in my stilettos.

People told me that "this is just how the childcare industry is," and "this is how it is working with all females." Someone also told me that I didn't "pay enough to have qualified staff."

Not only did I listen to them—I believed them. Surely there's been a time when you listened to someone else's opinions or beliefs and allowed them to dictate how you move and show up in the world. We've all been there, and when we do that, it prevents us from being our best and most authentic selves. In my case, it kept me from being an effective leader. I was shaky and barely standing in my stilettos!

There was a time I found myself coming undone in a dark closet in my office, trying to hide my tears as I wiped them with my sleeve. At the time, I was losing money in my business. I didn't have enough customers, and I felt like a failure. I had put my entire life savings into my passion, and yet I could not effectively run my business. I barely had a staff, and the employees I did have were not loyal. Instead, they were ungrateful, unmotivated, and disengaged. I wanted my employees to like me. I wanted them to care about me and about my business, but I didn't have a clue how to turn things around and create a positive work environment. I was falling down in my stilettos!

I lacked mentorship and the support of a tribe. And in order to achieve success, I knew that had to change. It was not an overnight fix. It took time to find those I could trust to guide me, to attract the right people for my staff, and to develop strategies to create a balanced, pleasant environment for employees to work in. But when I did, I found I was finally standing and developing balance in my stilettos!

My growth as a leader was not a straight line. The opinions of others continued to hinder me from catapulting my organization in a positive direction. At times, I was riddled with self-doubt, and even when I was making the right moves, I was second-guessing them.

We all have a tendency to allow others' perceptions to become our reality. We fall prey to the negativity spewed at us by people who have not walked one mile in our shoes. And sometimes, we simply assume others are thinking poorly of us, even when they're not. We train ourselves to believe others don't like us or they think we're incapable or undeserving of success. This false narrative is just that—false. By realizing this, I was able to stand and better balance in my stilettos!

I lived this disastrous life for years, until one day, I decided that, while this may be society's norm, it would no longer exist in my organization. I began making very nominal changes over a period of time, and in turn, my company's culture shifted for the better. And by the time it did, I was standing tall and balanced in my stilettos!

First, we implemented uniforms. It's well-known that the number of decisions you have to make while preparing for work impacts how you feel about showing up at all. With the implementation of uniforms, our employees no longer had to worry about what to wear. We figured it out for them!

We also granted PTO days for tenured employees, along with ways to earn time off for others. We provided supplemental insurance and a 401(k) plan, and we instituted numerous staff appreciation events and raises. With these new policies and benefits, we were able to transform our workplace culture into a place where employees were excited to be and work. As a result, they became more engaged and enthusiastic. In turn, it was easier for me to communicate with and depend on my staff.

Just like the assembly of your favorite stilettos, systematically stitching all of these components together taught me how to create a safe, happy place for my valuable employees, which is a key role of any effective and excellent leader. My organization changed when I stepped up in my role as CEO and made it my mission to shift the workplace culture with positivity and mindful changes.

Creating a culture that is in line with your visions and goals will ultimately have a positive impact on your organization. Start with small changes, like I did, and these changes will lead to huge transformations over time. Although it's difficult and takes time, you *can* stand up and find balance in your stilettos!

The Importance of a Company Mission

Aside from these small shifts I started out with, there are plenty of other factors that foster a positive, successful work environment. One is defining a company's mission and supplementing it with definitive goals to achieve this mission, which allows team members to collaborate and enjoy succeeding together.

Picture your entrepreneurial team on a boat. There is only one goal—SUCCESS! In order to get there, the entire team has to row in the same direction; otherwise, you'll end up going in circles, or even going nowhere at all.

The mission statement of a company is important. It summarizes and communicates to others what you do, as well as why and how you do it. It also conveys what motivated you to start a business in the first place.

When a company has a good mission statement, it not only inspires everyone involved, it also helps maintain focus and the navigation toward growth. You know you have a good mission statement when, at the end of each day, you're able to reflect and say, "Mission accomplished."

Here are a few examples of great mission statements (all from female-owned and operated companies):

- **Crystal Khalil, The Khalil Experience**: To foster a narrative that validates, confirms, and celebrates the value of women leaders around the globe.

- **Sandi Edgehill, Sandi's Edge**: To inspire women to discover their healthy body and spirit in order to access the gift of happiness and freedom that awaits them.

- **Sara Blakey, Spanx**: To reshape the way you get dressed, so you can shape the world!

- **Jessica Alba, The Honest Company**: So you don't have to choose between what works and what's good for you.

- **Venita Dell, Helping Young Mothers Mentor Inc.**: To enhance the economic and social well-being of pregnant young mothers and dads (if present) by one-on-one mentoring, providing health education, vocational training, and life improvement sessions for the betterment of her (and him), their baby, and the family health well-being.

All of these company statements focus on working toward the greater good through small choices and actions. Their mission is in place to provide a guide for employees and the general public to know what they do and understand why. Jasmine Henry says, "When you make the effort to inspire, the result can be just the boost your brand needs."

Leading the Team

The ideal leader will realize they cannot expand and grow a business without the aid of a talented, effective team. Leadership is not about micromanaging others; rather, it's about building relationships, creating a positive work environment, and inspiring everyone to work together to achieve a common goal.

Most think being a leader requires you to be well-liked. The truth is, being liked does not make you a great leader. Being the leader of an organization requires you to be *respected*. And often, it's easier to earn someone's respect than it is to get someone to like you.

In order to earn your employees' and customers' respect, you must lead your team with integrity and fairness at all times. I always share with others that integrity is doing the right thing even when no one is looking.

Throughout my first year in business, I was struggling. I had low enrollment, inadequate staffing, and I was barely able to make ends meet. It's at times like this when you are more likely to go against your values and integrity. It's times like this when you're more likely to find yourself in a compromising situation during which you need to make a value-based decision. That happened to me.

I was once approached by another childcare provider who was closing her childcare facility. She offered to refer her students to my facility. Initially, I thought that this would be exactly what I needed to fix my problem. I would have more students, which would then create more revenue, and as a result, I could hire better staff. As I worked with her to prepare for the transfer of students, she finally revealed that all paperwork would be forged and that she expected me to provide her with a weekly cut of my income as compensation for the increase in revenue. She also assured me that the children would never enter my center, because she would ensure that the attendance was submitted so that the agency could provide payment to me. So essentially, I would be cheating the state by illegally receiving payments for children that were not in my care. Once I understood all of the details and her motives, the negotiations came to a screeching halt. While I was struggling in my business, I was not willing to compromise my integrity and risk losing my business or being incarcerated.

At the time, I had three staff members and approximately twenty children enrolled at my childcare center. I wasn't where I wanted to be yet, but I was proud of my success and what it had taken to grow my company from one child to twenty. There was no hesitation on my part. I immediately declined and continued to focus on my own mission and growing my business.

In business, underhanded deals like this are struck every day. Thankfully, this woman was unable to penetrate my principles. I was already making things happen on my own, and her offer didn't hold much appeal once I understood the gravity of what she was suggesting. That said, there will be times when the wrong choice can be easy to make. Keep in mind that building a business and achieving success is not supposed to be easy. Don't take the easy road; take the one with twists, turns, and uphill stretches. You'll be prouder when you reach the top if you do.

You don't simply want an organization that runs. You want an organization that runs well. Just as some stilettos leave you with blisters and sore feet, while some are surprisingly comfortable considering the height, your decisions and the team you build will determine whether you're able to sprint through the entrepreneurial world or whether you'll fall down and stay down.

Developing a strong, successful business is like crafting a comfortable, durable shoe. You need high-quality materials, and one of your main materials should be integrity. It's usually worth it to splurge on a good pair of heels rather than opting for a cheap pair. Sure, on the outside, the cheap shoes look just as nice, but the quality is ultimately what's important when you're standing around in them all day or walking into an important executive meeting.

When faced with a business decision, there's always only one choice to make, and that's to lean in on your integrity and the values that you have established for your organization. Neither the cheap, easy route nor what these choices look like on the surface are what matter. It's the stability those decisions will create, as well as the preservation of your integrity and honesty, that will ensure your business can go the extra mile in the long run.

Creating a Culture of Empathy and Trust

Empathy and trust are two other important qualities an effective leader needs to possess. Having the ability to understand what an employee is experiencing and being able to provide the appropriate assistance builds trust, respect, and dedication.

Employees are humans, and all humans just want to be seen, just as I did when I worked for someone else. Your employees want to know that you understand them, and they want to feel like they matter. How you ensure that these needs are met is by practicing empathy. It should be a primary goal to always remember that your employees are people. Remember to stop and put yourself in their shoes from time to time. Taking the time to acknowledge them, their emotions, and their experiences reminds them that they are an integral part of your organization.

As a leader, it is your responsibility to listen to the ideas and concerns of staff members, and more than that, to be grateful that they are willing to share, whether what they have to say relates to the business or their personal lives.

If you are empathetic and genuine, the trust of your employees will follow. Trust is transactional. Earning your employees' trust isn't the bottom line. You, as their leader, want to be able to trust them too. When you're able to exchange trust with your employees, a bond is formed—human to human, employer to employee. This mutual understanding is invaluable when it comes to building your team.

This open line of communication will strengthen relationships within the organization, and as a result, your employees will become more invested in helping the company grow and succeed.

Bring Transparency Center Stage

Transparency is key to building trust, and multiple studies have shown that transparency is essential to employees. They want to feel confident that they are seeing the whole picture. When working at a company that is perceived as transparent, employees perform better. In contrast, companies that are perceived as nontransparent lack employee trust. An American Psychological Association survey found that an astonishing 1 in 4 employees do not trust their employer. Additionally, 1 in 2 employees feel that their company isn't being upfront with them, which leads to them remaining disconnected from the company's bigger vision.

Another study, this one from CareerBuilder, found that 37% of employees surveyed were likely going to quit their job because they were not confident in their boss's performance, and they had poor relationships with others in their work environment. Issues like these can be solved with honesty and open communication. Transparency within a company can build better relationships by encouraging sharing and trust in a judgment-free environment. Candid conversations, honest feedback, and even sharing bad news instead of keeping it under wraps can go a long way.

Be prepared to explain your decisions. Here is a minor example of bringing your employees in on your decision-making process. In my childcare facility, I always focus on professionalism, and one of the ways to display professionalism is for the staff to wear uniforms. I decided that my staff would wear khaki pants. I liked the neutral color, which would complement the company polo shirts. The staff, on the other hand, wanted to wear black pants. Instead of dismissing their opinion, I gave them the floor to explain their reasoning and then weighed the options again. Ultimately, I stuck with my original decision for the employee uniform, but I held a staff meeting to discuss my reasoning behind this decision. From a leadership perspective, I wanted the uniform to be easily monitored, and in the past, staff had worn black stretch pants or black leggings that were inappropriate for the workplace.

As a compromise, I agreed to observe Casual Friday. Although they were not happy about the khaki pants, my staff was elated to not wear uniforms on Fridays. I was transparent about my vision for the company and professional image for my staff, which led to a mutual understanding. In the end, this situation was not about what color pants we would wear. It was about everyone feeling like they had a voice.

Aside from improving relationships and increasing retention rates, a transparent company culture can also improve productivity. When employees understand all angles of the company's vision, they will feel more inspired and capable of fulfilling their day-to-day duties because they'll know how their job fits into the bigger picture.

Inspire Others

The most productive and dedicated employees are those who feel appreciated and valued. As individuals, we all crave connection with others, and we want to be a part of something bigger than ourselves. Therefore, as a leader, invest some time having meaningful conversations with employees. Your employees want to know that you really see them as individuals who play pivotal roles in your company, not just as cogs in the wheel.

I send each of my employees a simple handwritten note twice a year—on their birthday and on their anniversary with the company. The birthday cards are handmade and embellished, and I sign and address each one personally. The purpose of the anniversary note is to acknowledge their commitment to the organization and remind them of my gratitude that they choose to work for me rather than someone else. In my past, I would have loved receiving a card from my CEO expressing appreciation and thanking me for my contributions to the organization, so I enjoy doing this for my employees.

Taking a few brief moments to ask about your employee's weekend, recent vacation, or their new dog will go a long way in getting better acquainted with your team members. Sharing tidbits about yourself is just as important as listening, so they get to know you too. Make yourself accessible. Keeping your personal life entirely a mystery creates the image that you are above them, or separate. When people show interest *in one another*, it is perceived as caring, and in the workplace, this can be a great motivator for employees.

During these interactions, also share your vision for the business and the roles everyone will play in achieving these desired goals. Through these conversations, not only will your passion for business and success shine through, but you'll also be reminding your employees that you care about them and see their input concerning your business plans as valuable. Transparency and inclusion can be powerful tools for inspiring others and creating a strong work environment.

Stay True to a Clear Vision

Failure should never define you. Rather, it should help refine you. Every successful businesswoman recognizes setbacks and hurdles as tools for self-improvement and growth. It can be difficult to adopt this perspective at first. Setbacks and obstacles can certainly be frustrating, but when it comes down to it, the right company culture will both expect challenges and even welcome them as a means of improving and advancing.

I have helped many female entrepreneurs define their company vision and ensure that it is clear, concise, and in line with their personal aspirations and values. After defining this vision, the question often becomes: how do you stay on track when everything seems to be working against you?

The answer is having a clear vision and maintaining focus on it. Remember, how you envision your company's trajectory and ultimate achievements can act as your guide. Those hopes and dreams—that's where you want to be. Never lose sight of that.

During challenging times, your vision will help steer you in the right direction and motivate you because it will serve as a point of reference. You'll be able to measure your progress against your ultimate vision, and almost always, you'll see that you are making strides, even when it feels like you're not moving at all. Slow growth is still growth! Any progress is a step in the right direction.

Regularly check in with yourself and make sure that you're staying true to the company vision that you defined. Over time, you'll likely need to adapt this vision, but the important thing is that you don't lose sight of it, especially when times get tough. Stay true to yourself, because it's when times get tough that you are likely to cave and alter your vision and goals to be easier to attain or in a way that no longer reflects your original dreams.

"Leadership," Sheryl Sandberg, Chief Operating Officer of Facebook, says, "is about making others better as a result of your presence and making sure that impact lasts in your absence." It's up to you to decide what you want that impact to be and to never lose sight of it.

Invest in Leadership and Mentoring Efforts

Multiple studies, including those conducted by The Conference Board, Bersin & Associates, and McBassi & Company, have concluded that organizations that invest in leadership and mentorship initiatives perform better than those that don't.

Within a company, providing accessible leadership programs for your employees will greatly improve your team as a whole, as well as garner enthusiasm among your employees. Leadership development opportunities grow and expand on your team's existing talent, provide room for advancement, and keep the best employees around for the long haul as they see the opportunities for further education and advancement. Such programs will also help with recruitment efforts because the best candidates are looking for long-term opportunities and room for growth at the company that employs them.

Mentorship opportunities should also be common and open to employees at every level. Employees should ideally have the chance to be mentored, as well as the chance to mentor interns, new employees, and employees in other departments that are looking to make a new move in their career. These opportunities will engage your entire employee base while advancing their skill sets and promoting teamwork.

It's important that employees have a crystal-clear idea of exactly what it takes to advance within your company, as well as an understanding of the expectations of their role and anything they are trying to attain, including pay and benefits. On top of that, a great leader will provide clear paths for them to learn, advance, and achieve success within your company. If they want to grow, give them that opportunity. They'll be better for it, and so will you.

Cultivate Passion

Employees who become company advocates play a major role in both your consumer brand and your branding efforts, and sometimes, even employee retention. These are the people both inside and outside of your company who support your work. They are deeply passionate about your company, and they believe not only in your organizational values, but that you are actively and successfully working toward fulfilling your company's mission.

Passion is central to success. Passionate employees are motivated to do the work because it's fun, challenging, and rewarding. They do not work only for the benefits or to avoid punishment.

As you can imagine, the key to cultivating passion in others is being passionate about the cause yourself. Once others recognize your commitment to your company and the drive behind your mission, they'll get behind it, too. Then it's up to you to cultivate their passion through company events and other efforts on a regular basis. Keep that fire alive!

In my organization, there is no question that I believe in my employees or that I am interested in their success. The company covers all cost of training, employees are paid to attend training and transportation is provided if needed. For me, success is not just about *my* accomplishments; it's about my employees' accomplish - ments and being there to celebrate the growth and success of others. I am passionate about advancement and learning, and, in turn, they are too.

Furthermore, we share in the success of our company. When we're doing well, it brings joy to all. We truly believe that we are benefitting the public and making the world a better place with our services. This enthusiasm is enhanced when customers reflect this same passion. There is nothing better than devoted customers who believe so deeply in your service that they voluntarily spread the word on your behalf.

Passion is necessary for entrepreneurs. Maya Angelou said it best when she said, "My mission in life is not merely to survive, but to thrive, and to do so with some passion, some compassion, some humor, and some style." Remember, passion is contagious, and it starts from within.

Diversity and Inclusion Drive Success

When leaders and organizations embrace the assets of a diverse and inclusive company and staff, the resulting success is phenomenal.

It is important to create a workplace culture that utilizes and celebrates individual strengths and talents. Making it a priority to have diversity and inclusion in leadership and the workplace creates a space in which a variety of people, along with their ideas, gifts, opinions, and assets are recognized and encouraged, regardless of education, background, or demographics. This form of leadership creates unification among many people from different walks of life, which creates a major advantage over the competition.

Diversity among your team members opens your company up to the world. Having hundreds of eyes that see the world from a different vantage point is invaluable when it comes to marketing and customer outreach. Your customers are different, and your team members should be too. More than that, a diverse workplace is a fun one to be a part of. Consider how little we'd learn day to day or how one-dimensional we would be if we were all the same!

Be Driven by Customer Success

A leader recognizes that customer success and satisfaction are top priorities. Every aspect of a company affects the customer, whether it's the processes and systems, or the marketing and product creation.

Being methodical, aware, and taking extra care ensures customers are satisfied with the products and services you provide. By involving all departments and holding individuals accountable, everyone is motivated to consider how their actions, performance, and attitude affect and make the customer feel and respond. A primary goal of your company should be building relationships with your customers and clients and winning their loyalty.

In any business, including my childcare center, it can seem like an arduous task to involve everyone and keep them on the same page. But when all employees in an organization believe in the mission and the values of the company, this becomes more manageable.

Our clientele consists of children and families, and our goal is to provide quality care. Everyone has a job to do, all while keeping these specific customers in mind. My staff understands their individual responsibilities and how they fit in achieving customer success, and furthermore, the overall success of the organization. The kitchen staff is responsible for making sure that nutritious food is ordered, prepared, and served warm. Our teachers ensure that we have quality programming and positive family engagement. And our leadership staff makes sure that our staff and families are happy and that the center is financially viable so that we can continue to provide the best care for our families and their children. Our actions, attitudes, and aim for top-notch service are what gains us loyal clientele and attracts new customers.

In my consulting agency, on the other hand, I am a team of one. So I, personally, am responsible for knowing my client and providing the correct services to help them meet their business needs. While this operation runs differently, the basics are the same. My actions and attitude drive my customers' behaviors. If I focus on them and their needs, the services I provide as a result of that focus satisfies them and attract others to seek my services.

Provide Employee Support

As a leader, your days will be filled with addressing an array of many different matters, including problem-solving, attending meetings, and delegating responsibilities. At times, you'll be stretched pretty thin; however, it is imperative that your team knows you're there to support them, no matter what your workday brings.

Always seek opportunities to energize and motivate your team, provide them with ample opportunities to shine by giving them assignments, offer training that will further their knowledge and abilities, and create a better equipped and informed organization.

Overall, as a transformational leader, your focus should always be on treating everyone as an equal, communicating clearly and consistently, building relationships, inspiring everyone, setting realistic goals, and recognizing achievements. Strive to foster a healthy workplace culture, which will serve as the sturdy cast around your entire organization, much like the counter of your stiletto, which provides shape and support to the entire shoe, as well as to your foot within it.

EMPLOYEE EXPERIENCE

Employees are an integral part of any successful business, and two of the biggest challenges in constructing the perfect team are attracting and retaining the right people.

According to research conducted by Gallup in 2018, a mere 34% of employees felt engaged at work, which equates to a lot of discontent staff members who are likely looking for another job.

Unhappy employees can contribute to a toxic work environment and can disrupt morale. On the other hand, employees who do feel engaged are more productive, healthier, motivated to excel, and committed to their work, which in turn increases customer success.

If the tips of your stilettos are too wide, the additional space allows friction to blister your skin. On the other hand, if your stilettos have narrow tips, your toes will ache walking around all day thanks to the lack of room. Ill-fitting shoes are simply not comfortable. Your employees can be uncomfortable in your organization as well. Employees want to see how they fit perfectly into the organization. Equally important to fitting in, employees need room to grow and advance. It's your job to establish their essential roles within your company, make them feel at home, and set them up for additional learning opportunities, growth, and advancement.

Creating a positive employee experience is imperative, and you can guarantee a positive work experience for your employees with a few straightforward processes that communicate that you care about their future, productivity, and well-being.

Leading and Sustaining Peak Performance

In addition to providing an amiable work environment, a good leader needs to motivate employees to perform well on a consistent basis. Naturally, everyone will have an occasional off day when they're not performing at the top of their game, but otherwise, the steps below will help in sustaining peak performance.

1. Clarify Expectations

For the most part, employees want to do a great job, but in order to do so, they must have a clear understanding of what is expected of them. Commit to setting realistic goals for all employees and clarifying how their individual responsibilities fit into the big picture. Provide information and encourage your employees to come to you with additional questions.

It's also important to identify how varying levels of performance will be recognized or compensated. While dedicated employees take pride in their work regardless, communicating what's in it for them helps motivate them to succeed. You should want to reward those working for you when they perform well.

2. Provide Feedback

It's beneficial to have conversations regarding performance and expectations regularly. Employees will become acclimated to this process, and routine feedback promotes accountability within a supportive environment.

As their leader, this will give you the opportunity to reward and commend good work, as well as provide constructive criticism when necessary to help those employees grow. Checking in means your employees will feel connected, and this will benefit the workplace culture more than you know.

Regular performance reviews will generate trust among coworkers as well. It's not uncommon for there to be a weak link, whether that's an employee who is falling behind and needs a helping hand or someone who has a poor work ethic and little respect for their role and the company as a whole. When employees feel like they are working harder than their coworkers who are reaping the same benefits, this creates hostility. When it feels like this goes unacknowledged by their superiors, that resentment doubles. Making it your priority to check in on your employees' performance nips scenarios like this in the bud.

3. Nurture Relationships

Strong relationships between leaders and employees help build trust and respect. This isn't a matter of simply liking each other or getting along. Generally, when you hire someone, the hope is that they stick around for a long time. In order for that to happen, you must first value your relationships with your employees and then maintain them.

Within a company, you will spend as much time with the other people who work there, if not more, than your family. Being coworkers is a fairly intimate relationship. You work closely and, ultimately, bond.

The relationship between a superior and an employee is similar to two coworkers, but there is more trust necessary because of the power dynamic involved. As the leader, it's your responsibility to foster and grow these relationships. The relationship between a boss and an employee takes a bit more maintenance, too, because depending on everyone's role, you may not be working directly with your employees every day. These connections can be nurtured by:

- Communicating in a tone that is uplifting and supportive

- Acknowledging accomplishments verbally

- Rewarding employees with gift cards, bonuses, or pay increases

- Letting employees know you have confidence in their abilities and you trust them to achieve their goals

Valuing Your Employees

Making employees feel valued isn't difficult, but it does require some attention to detail. Overall, it requires taking time to connect, celebrating the small things, and providing employees with the necessary tools to get the job done.

- **Personalize It:** Just like in a personal relationship, the little things can make a big difference for employees. Acknowledging employees for a job well done is important. Occasionally, it may be in the form of a quick thank you, but opting to send a handwritten note that includes specifics about their skills and successes can go a long way in making an employee feel valued.

- **Improve the Workspace:** Create a comfortable, cheerful work area for employees. The design and furnishings of a space can drastically improve a person's experience while working in it. Your employees are spending more of their time awake in this space you create for them than in their own homes. Ensure that they are equipped with items that will help them perform optimally, such as up-to-date technology, ergonomic furniture and accessories, improved lighting, and accessible climate control. On a smaller scale, consider a lounge area or complimentary snacks in the break room.

- **Give Them Ownership:** By giving ownership of specific tasks that allow employees to use their talents, you're not only empowering them with your trust, but you're also encouraging them to grow. No one likes to be micromanaged. By handing projects off and not hovering, you are signaling that you find that particular employee competent and good at their job.

Provide Professional Development

Whether you have a team of talented, productive, dedicated employees or a group of novices, it is vital that you provide opportunities for professional development.

Even the most capable employee can become complacent, which can negatively impact your bottom line. There's always room to learn new methodologies, improve skills, or increase performance. Learning is something that should never stop—for you or your staff.

There are multiple forms of training—on-the-job training, online training, mentoring sessions, and individual professional development, to name a few. Rather than viewing it as an expense, consider it an investment in your most valuable asset—your employees. Giving employees access to training and implementing strategies to ensure follow-through will not only benefit your business production, but it will also enhance your brand and reputation and boost employee morale.

Recognize Good Performance

Most of us can relate to putting our all into something, only to go without recognition for our hard work. In fact, the 2014 TINYpulse Employee Engagement and Organizational Culture Report found that an incredible 79% of employees feel undervalued. Many employees feel like they go above and beyond their duties and receive nothing in return. This leads to bitterness within the workplace and to employees feeling drained and ignored. It can also lead to burnout, when an employee begins to wonder if their hard work is really worth it.

As the CEO of your organization, it is important that you treat all of your employees fairly. This will increase trust and respect. You must make sure all of your employees are in the right seat and that they know, understand, and are a fit for their role in your organization. This will help them to better manage their workload and feel a sense of accomplishment. You must communicate effectively as a leader, and you should always communicate from a point of empathy and understanding. Even in the worst situations, make sure to communicate with others in a way that leaves their dignity intact. As the saying goes, you will catch more flies with honey than with vinegar.

When these systems are in place, employee recognition becomes easy to do and an ingrained part of the culture of your organization. Recognizing employees who exhibit initiative and drive will increase retention and attract employees who want to work for a company that will value them and that has an excellent employee recognition program in place.

Employees should be incentivized for consistently showing up, getting things done, and acting as a proud face of your company. Recognizing every employee for their ongoing effort, commitment, and accomplishments will keep them engaged, improve retention and overall loyalty, and inspire your hardest workers to keep doing their best.

Making sure that your employees don't feel neglected or lost among the other employees will make a positive difference in their happiness and contribution. Don't give them a chance to feel crowded in the tip of the stiletto amidst the daily operations.

A Glassdoor study revealed that more than 80% of employees admit that the appreciation of their superiors motivates them to work harder. And even with this knowledge, less than 9% of highly engaged organizations recognize employees for doing a good job, Bonusly reports.

Of course, the key to successfully recognizing and cultivating good performance is awareness. While 3 out of every 4 companies have an employee recognition program of some sort, only 58% of employees are aware of their company's recognition initiatives.

Recognizing your employees is an opportunity to have fun and be creative. Each December, we have an all-expenses-paid holiday celebration. We use this time to come together as an organization to celebrate our success for the year and unwind over dinner. During this time, we dress up, strap on our stilettos, have an enjoyable time, and even give out awards and trophies. The awards include the Spirit Award, which is awarded to the person who has the best team spirit. The Fashion Award—that goes to the most fashionable person. There's also the Energizer Bunny Award, which goes to the employee with endless energy, and more. The employees and I look forward to it, and a fun time is had by everyone.

Your Role in Onboarding

Onboarding is the process of integrating a new employee into a company and familiarizing them with the work environment and procedures. As a leader, you should view onboarding as an opportunity to get acquainted with a new employee. Dedicating time to discuss the company culture yourself rather than delegating it to someone else will actively display your interest in creating an inclusive culture for everyone in your organization.

However, if time constraints do not allow for this initial one-on-one time, there are other options for the onboarding process. For instance, you might consider onboarding multiple people during a single meeting or training session, or constructing an email that includes your photo, a brief bio, and a snippet of the company vision along with a warm welcome.

Onboarding is your new employee's first impression of the company, and instead of simply addressing the checklist of new hire paperwork, this process should involve helping the new employee feel like a part of the team.

The onboarding process will look different for every organization. Some may last one day, others may last a week. When I first started out in business, I didn't have an onboarding process. Honestly, I didn't even know what onboarding was from the perspective of providing the experience for my staff. Eventually, after significant turnover, it hit me that not only did my employees not understand what my company stood for, they also didn't understand or buy into my vision. They didn't understand my expectations. Some of them didn't know how to properly do their job, and one of them didn't even know that I owned the company!

I'd expected them to meet all of my expectations without giving them a comprehensive introduction to my company and their role within it. I started with a very simple onboarding process. It lasted one day. Today, we have a systematic and structured onboarding process that lasts two weeks, and as a result, we have increased employee morale and decreased turnover.

Not having a solid onboarding experience translates to a loss of revenue. Investopedia reports that "not every new hire will demand the same process, but even an $8 an hour employee can end up costing a company around $3,500 in turnover costs, both direct and indirect." These costs include things like recruiting, training, materials, and other resources.

If I had known to implement a proper onboarding process sooner, I would have saved a lot of money. I originally thought the only cost associated with recruiting would be posting a job ad. I soon learned that it included so much more. In the childcare industry, turnover is certain and, most times, inevitable. Often, by the time I hired and trained an employee, I would lose them, sometimes without even a two-week notice, and I'd find myself right back in the same hiring hamster wheel. I've lived and learned, and now, I take pleasure in teaching my clients how to effectively onboard in their businesses in order to avoid the same mistakes I made. I assist them in creating a solid onboarding system, including recruiting, hiring, onboarding, and firing.

Why You Should Seek and Implement Feedback

The word *feedback* often has a negative connotation; however, feedback is pivotal in helping leaders make better-informed decisions, facilitating employee and leadership improvement, and enhancing the work environment.

1. Employee Insight

As leaders, we rely on our employees to handle various tasks, and as such, they can provide firsthand feedback on the goings-on in the company on a routine basis. A great leader welcomes input from staff members of all levels. This insight can aid in your decision-making process. Those to whom you delegate can, in turn, make it easier for you to see the clear picture you would not otherwise see without their feedback.

Also, when you are in a leadership role, it's not uncommon for there to be distance between you and the workroom floor. That's why it is invaluable to have trust in your capable employees, who can be your eyes and provide astute feedback. These employees may even be more equipped to make suggestions or decisions than you are at times.

Plus, when employees know that they are being heard and trusted, they will be that much more engaged at work. In fact, Salesforce Research found that employees who feel heard at work are 4.6 times more motivated to do their best work. This means that listening to your employees and collecting their feedback is a win-win in every sense. You get the information, and they feel included.

2. Corrective Feedback

In an environment where feedback is encouraged, feedback is not as likely to appear as criticism. Corrective feedback helps employees make the necessary changes to improve their performance, and it is absolutely necessary in cultivating the most efficient staff possible. It's best to encourage a nonjudgmental, feedback-focused work environment from the very beginning.

When you have something you'd like them to work on or improve, learning how to give constructive feedback is essential if you want to empower your employees without anyone feeling called out or ridiculed. Like I mentioned earlier, regular performance reviews are a great way to provide feedback to your employees during a private, scheduled conversation. This way, none of their coworkers are privy to what is discussed, and because your employee is already anticipating their performance review, they will not feel ambushed.

Tracking their progress and acknowledging the strides they make to address your feedback is also a huge part of your employee's success. Not only does this motivate them, but it also confirms that you believe in their ability to improve, rather than providing feedback simply to cover your bases and then letting them go down the line.

3. Employee Feedback

Feedback in the workplace shouldn't just go one way. Aside from collecting employee feedback on company goals and initiatives, you should also seek feedback on your performance and ask what you can do better as a leader. After all, even the most experienced leader has room for improvement.

When one of my past employees turned in her two-week notice, the conversation turned into an unsolicited, though enlightening, exit interview. She suggested that I needed a mentor. I was shocked! I thought that I was doing a great job. This particular employee liked me as a person but didn't feel like my company was a good fit for her. She felt employee relations were combative, and she thought that some of the obstacles I faced trying to run my organization would not be an issue for someone with more experience, or if someone more experienced mentored me. At that time, she offered up the name of a woman who had been doing childcare for over thirty years and provided me with her contact information.

Initially, I rejected this suggestion of finding a coach or mentor. Even though I was overwhelmed, in a constant state of sleep deprivation, and had gained a lot of weight from stress, I still believed I was perfectly capable of running my business successfully. And I was capable, but I didn't have the knowledge and experience that I do today. I still had a lot to learn. It was my ego thinking, and I let my ego call the shots until years later, when I found myself at a point where I'd made it as far as I could go without additional knowledge, insight, resources, and experience, and I knew that I needed help. Once I opened myself up to learning from others and growing my skill set and knowledge, I was able to grow my business, more than doubling my income and my customer base.

By giving your employees the opportunity to provide you with honest feedback, you gain a better understanding of how they perceive you, and you are challenged to be better, just as you challenge them. Like I mentioned earlier, your employees want to feel valued. Asking them how you, their boss, can improve does this and more. You are being vulnerable and showing them that you are willing to change to make their experience better.

Cultivating an environment in which your employees are comfortable providing feedback openly is ideal. Being able to converse on a human level with each of your employees without them feeling the need to censor themselves is essential for long-term success. If you have cultivated a culture of honesty and respect, employees will be more likely to provide feedback. That said, many people feel uncomfortable scoring their superiors or providing entirely honest feedback unless it is anonymous. This is a common method of collecting performance feedback.

Keep in mind that leading by example is one of the best ways to motivate your employees to learn and improve. By requesting feedback on your performance, showing interest in how others view your leadership skills, taking the feedback in stride, and making diligent efforts to remedy any concerns and to improve in the suggested areas, you motivate your employees to take as much pride in their work and make improvements if needed.

Flexibility

The average workplace today is quite different than it once was. We move at a much faster pace, and in general, we are more flexible. It's important as a CEO to understand your employees and what motivates them, and to consider what they have going on outside the workplace.

The employee experience begins with the first contact, and as the leader of your organization, it's up to you to ensure it's a positive one from day one—from workplace culture and conditions to relationships, goals, compensation, and development opportunities.

We know that happy employees work more efficiently and provide higher returns on investment (ROI) for businesses, large and small.

A facet of leading a diverse and inclusive organization is recognizing that the traditional nine-to-five day doesn't work for everyone. Family dynamics vary greatly among a diverse group of employees—think single adults, newlyweds, parents, or children of aging parents.

What I consider a comfortable pair of shoes, you might not, and this also goes for what we consider an ideal work schedule. Flexibility and choices are a must to improve productivity and efficiency. Today, we have the capability to allow staff to work varying hours, rearrange schedules, and even work remotely. The more flexibility you offer in employee scheduling, the more respect and loyalty you'll gain from your employees. This is because offering choices demonstrates that you know work is not their life, just a small part of it. It's important to show that you value your staff and their personal lives outside of work. You would want someone to do this for you too! Not only will this flexibility enhance performance, but it will also reduce absenteeism and increase employee engagement.

Understanding and enhancing the employee experience is a major leveraging tool against the competition. Flexibility can greatly enhance the experience within your organization, and it is attractive to potential candidates when recruiting. Gallup reports that 54% of office workers would leave their job for one that offers more flexibility. This is important to modern-day employees. In addition to attracting the right talent, flexibility will also play a major role in retaining them.

The way we work is changing, and a positive employee experience enhances business success. That's the bottom line.

Invest in Technology

Keeping on top of technological developments is a must when running any kind of business. With so many innovations in recent years, staying on top of the tech space can give you a competitive edge, so long as you invest in the right tools.

From software to hardware, the types of technology you need to invest in will vary depending on the type of work you do. For instance, many companies have benefited from investments in 3D printing technology, which can help with everything from real-world production to prototyping. Meanwhile, other companies are commonly utilizing renewable energy, the internet of things (IoT), and remote-working software.

Technology is such an important investment for today's companies that American Express estimates that IT accounts for roughly 19% of business expenditure.

Investing in the right technology can ultimately save your company time. For example, investing in cloud collaboration and management tools like Asana and Trello could increase productivity by an astounding 20%. The right tech investments could also improve security, which is of major importance for today's consumers. On top of that, emerging technologies can help you stand out while better understanding and engaging with your customer base.

As a new entrepreneur, it was difficult for me to find money to invest in technology. I was only thinking of my business in the moment and not focusing on growth and long-term success. As entrepreneurs, we sometimes avoid certain practices that, once implemented, can help us save money that can be used to fund necessities, like useful technology.

There are programs and applications out there that I encourage others to take advantage of, and some of them are free! While it takes some trial and error to find your fit, there are programs for any type of business. Over the years, I've taken to using Remind, which allows me to communicate with staff and customers via text messaging. Brightwheel helps me keep track of enrollment and student ratios, and Wave allows me to take payments and keep track of my accounting.

These free services have allowed me to create organized systems that benefit workplace communication, enrollment, and finances, and the only cost was time invested in learning the systems. As your organization grows, so will your technology needs. I now use BambooHR for human resource management and QuickBooks for financial accounting.

While it may seem like investing in technology is solely a profit-driven decision, it supports your staff as well. We all enjoy using cutting-edge technology in the workplace and at home. More than that, providing the best technology for your employees ensures they have the tools they need to do their best work, often more efficiently.

SYSTEMS

Implementing the proper systems in your business will allow you to successfully manage your team and their performance, maintain business finances, and have processes in place for the various day-to-day operations. While this systematization is not a fast process, it is doable and critical.

A business system is designed to streamline the processes and operations of a specific area of your organization. This system utilizes common methodologies and tools to create an effective process that takes into account potential problems. A collection of efficient business systems work together to support a steady workflow and work toward the achievement of the overarching company mission.

You may think that you are not currently qualified to implement executable systems in your business, not realizing that you've been doing this all along in some aspect of your life.

Almost all of us have been to school, which requires managing a daily schedule, transportation, friendships and frenemies, homework, and extracurricular activities. As an adult, you likely have systems in place to balance work, physical wellness, hobbies, and a social life. If you're a mom, you're working to balance all of these, along with meeting the demands of your growing children, including providing nutritious meals, keeping up with their school lives, and managing their well-being.

I can easily relate. As a single parent, I found myself overwhelmed by all of the demands I was confronted with on a daily basis. The expectations of being a good mom and making sure my children's basic needs were met, getting them to school on time, helping with homework, and taking them to extracurricular activities with sports and friends was a full-time job. Plus, I was juggling motherhood with getting to work on time every day, managing my home, and trying to take care of myself. As women, we have a tendency to take on more than we can handle and then downplay how difficult it is to manage our daily lives while holding our households together. For some reason, our goal is to make it look easy when it's anything but.

Have you ever taken a moment to pat yourself on the back for how well you're able to make this seemingly insurmountable combination of tasks seem effortless, all while strutting around in your stilettos, dressed for work, or running around in sneakers before or after a trip to the gym? If you haven't, you've got my permission to do so now.

These skills—multitasking, managing routine, punctuality, considering others, and functioning well under pressure—are needed to run a successful business. This is why I believe so strongly that women are meant to be leaders. They are innately equipped to steer the ship and keep it afloat. They are superheroes—strong enough to snap on their capes and accomplish their daily tasks while balancing life and running around in stilettos.

So remember, if you exist on this earth, you already have systems in place, and they are designed to do exactly what you've put them in place to do. As individuals, what works for one person doesn't necessarily work for the next. The same goes for businesses, and as a leader, it's up to you to figure out what systems will support and fit your business. This is a big responsibility because, within an organization, there are many people your chosen systems will affect.

Having no system is a system. An ineffective system is a system. And a solid, well-planned, well-designed program that supports your company's outcomes is a system as well.

Having key business systems in place is essential to a strong foundation and steady, never-ending growth. Each of the systems listed in this section work to provide accurate reporting, excellent customer care, ideal employee experience, and a business that operates smoothly and efficiently. The collar of your stiletto forms the rim of the shoe and encases your foot. An organization can exist without a strong set of business systems in place, but it will not run as efficiently, feel as comfortable, or fit your needs. Like the stitching of the collar of your stiletto, weaving key business systems that suit your company mission will hold your organization together.

Let's take a look at the key systems for any business.

Task Management

Task management is the handling of a task from beginning to end. Whether the tasks are related to marketing, planning, individual or departmental goals, task management will improve organization, processes, and prioritization.

Follow these tips to become a pro at task management:

1. **Identify tasks:** In order to get things done, you must first recognize what needs to be done.

2. **Track and update progress:** You'll struggle to make progress unless you are measuring it.

3. **Set reminders and deadlines:** Deadlines are important. In order to stay on track, there should be time constraints surrounding each task. The goal should be consistent effort, not complacency.

4. **Prioritize tasks:** Take a few minutes to look at what needs to be done each day and what is upcoming. Make sure time isn't being spent on tasks that are lower priority than others.

5. **Get rid of tasks that aren't important:** When something isn't important to your overall goal, don't waste time or resources on it.

6. **Break the larger tasks into small ones:** Large tasks with multiple layers can easily overwhelm you. Break them up into small and achievable tasks. Ultimately, you'll be doing the same work, just in smaller, more manageable doses. Shavings make a pile!

7. **Set boundaries and guard your time:** Your time is precious, so spend it on things that truly matter and will benefit your ultimate goals.

8. **Schedule time for tasks:** Designate time each day for specific tasks. Scheduling ahead of time creates accountability, as well as less chance for distraction or interruption.

9. **Communicate your expectations:** When assigning tasks, make sure you provide clear guidelines and encourage questions. Set deadlines and ensure your employees understand how you want them to prioritize their tasks. Once you master managing your own tasks, share task management tips with your employees.

A variety of task management software applications are available to enhance collaboration and focus, but the traditional manual processes, like tracking things with pen and paper, work also. Figure out what works best for you.

Time Management

We all have twenty-four hours in a day, but have you ever noticed that some people accomplish a lot more than others in those twenty-four hours? The key is time management. This is an incredibly important skill and should be taught across the entirety of business culture.

Here are four tips to improve time management for you and your team:

1. **Set Realistic Goals:** First, establish your goals and write them down. Once you do, you'll have the ability to track progress and maintain focus. Then, evaluate what is realistic to take on depending on your skill level or current workload. Set realistic deadlines for each task.

2. **Prioritize:** It's easy to stay busy, but without prioritizing tasks, being busy may not be beneficial in accomplishing all of your goals. Prioritize by deadline or importance, and put these tasks at the top of your list. Don't focus on tasks at random or by level of difficulty. By prioritizing your list of tasks, you'll steadily make progress and meet all deadlines.

3. **Make Plans:** Planning ahead prevents stress, saves time, and provides clarity on what needs to be accomplished to meet specific deadlines. Plan your days in advance and have routine meetings with your team to discuss goals and deadlines.

4. **Delegate**: It's not uncommon for someone in a leadership position to wear multiple hats in the business, taking on a variety of tasks as a way to stretch the budget. However, in order to expand your business, it is imperative that you delegate tasks. As a leader, your focus should be on planning for future success rather than spending valuable time performing day-to-day operations that others are capable of. Also, by delegating tasks to employees, you display your trust and confidence in them.

Delegating is a skill. As a leader, it's typical to feel like you should have a full plate and be extremely busy. It doesn't come naturally to some to hand off tasks, but spending time on tasks that can be easily handled by someone else will slow your progress and detract from other important work. Get comfortable delegating. You'll be glad you did.

Key Business Metrics

Business metrics are statistics that provide a clear picture of how well your company is performing. Also referred to as key performance indicators (KPI), these values help you determine what changes need to be made, as well as what areas are thriving.

When you work for someone else, your role and your department's role will affect certain aspects of the business metrics of the organization. A leader's relationship with business metrics is much different. As the CEO, you are responsible for every metric related to your organization's success. The key metrics that are tracked, as well as how many are tracked, vary from company to company. This depends on the size and type of your business.

Some examples of commonly tracked key business metrics are:

- Customer loyalty and retention

- Customer acquisition cost

- Sales revenue

- Sales growth

- Average profit margin

- Overhead costs

- Operating productivity and efficiency

- Employee turnover

- Employee engagement

- Social Media engagement

What you measure and track, you are able to improve.

Starting my consulting business had always been my dream. Now that I have, my hurdle has been social media. It's hard for me to share my life with the world, but today, that is a great way to find and connect with others. So, little by little, I began coming out of my shell. At first, the results were discouraging. I wasn't getting many "likes" or engagement on my posts. As a part of my KPIs, I started to track my weekly analytics. This helped me see the big picture and understand the world of social media. Tracking my weekly analytics taught me when to post, what to post, who my audience was, and what my audience liked, based on who was already responding to and interacting with my content. Equipped with this knowledge, I changed my social media tactics, and soon, with each post, my percentages increased, and my engagement improved.

There is software available that tracks key business metrics. In some cases, you will be required to do this on paper or create your own system. There is no right or wrong way to track metrics, but it's imperative that you do it. The ability to track, see, and analyze the financial health of your business is invaluable for improving and continuing upward trajectories and also preventing declines in your business.

Financial Management

When you have a good financial management system in place, you'll know how well your business is doing financially and why. Business is affected by every aspect, from employee attitudes and sales fluctuation to a change in cash flow or unexpected vendor delays, and it's important to track these metrics to ensure your business is operating optimally, as well as keeping on top of potential downturns that could harm your business.

Your financial management system could be as simple as having a spreadsheet and a bank account. Or it could be more robust, with a team of financial specialists, including a tax accountant, a bookkeeper, a banker, and a financial manager. Your financial management system often depends on the type and size of the business.

A financial management system will provide the information relevant for obtaining investors and loans, and also alert you to concerns so you can be proactive rather than reactive. With financial statements, inventory status, expenses, income, and profit values at your fingertips, you will avoid surprises that could be detrimental to your success.

Just as our vital readings are indicative of our overall health, what is reflected in your business's financial reports indicates the health of your business. And it's the healthy businesses that grow and succeed.

Change Management

A change management system is the process through which you introduce and enact an organizational change within your company, focusing on the people side of things. A smooth change management system will enhance your ability to stay competitive and make adjustments to address the ever-changing needs and demands of your customers and industry.

In March of 2020, my business, along with the world, was introduced to COVID-19. This virus necessitated many swift changes in our business model and how we served children and families each day. Teachers had to take extra precautionary measures to remain safe from contracting the virus. We had to increase our sanitizing and cleaning schedules to maintain a germ-free environment. We also had to send all children home who displayed any sign of cold or flu.

Aside from the health concern, the pandemic had a swift, negative impact on my business. Having fewer students meant a significant decrease in revenue, which meant I was not able to cover salaries. I needed to make immediate changes overnight. I quickly accessed our customers' needs and found out what our enrollment would be during this time. I then determined how many hours each employee needed or if they wanted to take advantage of time off. With that information, I created a schedule to accommodate both. As a result, our families received care, the staff was able to work enough to support their households, and our sanitary practices protected anyone in our facility from contracting the virus.

While this was a temporary change to meet the challenges of a global crisis, it was still a combination of changes I was required to implement smoothly using change management practices. It wasn't long before I again braced for and prepared my staff for more change that would be implemented when I had to close both facilities due to low enrollment, which led to more expenses than income.

Change management helps businesses identify irrelevant processes or issues with current operations and allows them to improve on an ongoing basis by making the implementation of change seamless.

In general, a change management system is comprised of these steps:

1. **Identify and Define the Desired Change**: Identify the necessary change and the reasoning behind it. Compare the current state to the future state that will result from this change. Announce this change to employees ahead of time and allow them to ask questions and voice concerns.

2. **Build a Team**: Build a team of talent that is enthusiastic about the upcoming change and capable of guiding and

communicating with others to carry out the actual work. This team will support the leader in enacting the desired change.

3. **Form a Vision and Strategies:** Create a plan of action and lay out new processes and operations needed for desired change. Communicate intentions and plans with employees. Dispel hesitation and spread enthusiasm. Make sure employees feel involved and on board with the new vision.

4. **Remove Barriers:** Remove ineffective processes and policies that do not benefit the company and that conflict with the new vision and desired changes.

5. **Enact Change:** Implement the planned change. Ensure all employees receive proper training and feel confident working within the change.

6. **Monitor:** Utilize KPI reporting and employee feedback to gauge the effectiveness of the change. Draw correlations between positive shifts in organizational success and share this with the staff. Success will motivate employees to sustain the change. Enthusiasm surrounding the change will ensure that it replaces previous operations.

Although change is inevitable in the business world, people are often resistant to change. This is normal, and it's why you need to ensure confidence is instilled in your staff early on, and they get on board. It's also why, as I've mentioned several times before, your employees need to feel involved and that they have a voice. The more typical change becomes in your business, and the more frequently you utilize a change management system to implement these changes, the easier it will be to maintain employee satisfaction and beat the competition.

Crisis Management

Fifty-nine percent of businesses have experienced a crisis, yet only 54% have a crisis management plan.

Planning for a potential crisis is one of the simplest ways to prevent or overcome a crisis. Being a few steps ahead should always be the goal. Potential crises include, for example, a data breach, employee misconduct, recurring customer service issues, or a pandemic. Problems like these can harm your company's reputation and more. Through effective crisis management, you'll be able to anticipate potential issues, identify risks, and create a process for appropriately responding.

One spring day, around 1 p.m., the children were sleeping on their cots. It was storming outside, and all was peaceful as the rain hit against the windows. That is until, all of a sudden, rain came pouring into the room from the ceiling as the children slept. In a panic, my staff and I rushed to get all of the children to a dry space downstairs while the top floor flooded with dirty, murky, foul-smelling water. I was terrified and in tears. There was a flooded room above our heads, my staff and children were not safe, and I didn't know what this would mean for my business.

I had to close for a week, and during that time, I looked for a new location. Luckily, I did not lose any of my staff members or customers, and within three months, I was able to move into a larger facility with better amenities and a roof that was sealed and did not leak.

I learned that it would take a lot more than a little bit of water to drown my dreams. This predicament was not just a test for my business, but a test of personal growth and crisis management skills. I was tested as an entrepreneur. Instead of running for cover, instead of hiding, and instead of quitting, I stepped up and faced to the challenge head-on.

As female entrepreneurs, we have to get up, stand up, strap on our stilettos, tie on our capes, grab a raincoat, and an umbrella, and weather the storm. Maintain your focus on growing your organization, and don't be naïve to think issues won't arise. And most importantly, remember that the rainbow always comes after the storm!

In general, crisis management is comprised of four phases:

1. **Preparation:** Anticipate and predict what risks your business faces. Assess the organization's weaknesses. Identify effective plans of action for each potential risk. Prepare measures such as communication methods, chain of command, emergency funds, and a crisis manager. Test prevention plans and reevaluate based on weaknesses.

2. **Response:** Assess the situation and company needs and work to meet those needs. Assess your public message. Respond to the media. Ensure the crisis does not linger. Prevent additional damage.

3. **Stabilization:** Perform an investigation, if necessary. Handle those at fault, if applicable. Communicate with and reassure staff. Monitor the situation and take additional measures, if needed, to support your initial response.

4. **Recovery:** Consider necessary changes to staff or operations following the crisis. Determine what ongoing monitoring is needed. Rework this particular crisis into your existing crisis management plan.

NAVIGATING THE GLASS CEILING

As a female entrepreneur, you're likely familiar with the "glass ceiling." If not, it is a reference to the invisible barrier to professional advancement that women face in the workplace. This includes roadblocks ahead of equal pay, acquiring positions in the top levels of organizations, promotions, raises, and in general, receiving professional respect. Sadly, this glass ceiling is still part of the architecture in today's average workplace and in business.

The shank of a stiletto is the bridge between the heel and sole of the shoe and supports the arch of the foot. It helps to carry the load and provides reinforcement and stability. By championing yourself when others won't, staying true to your passion to serve others and achieve success, and standing tall in the face of adversity, you can be your own support. While it may be unfair, the truth is, women must work twice as hard in the workplace to gain the same recognition as their counterparts. Accept this and press on. Being your best self is the only tool you need to build your own shank to success. Make sure that, like your favorite part of stilettos, it can carry the load.

I am someone who prides myself on continually working on my professional development. I completed college in a nontraditional fashion. Furthermore, I completed three college degrees in about the same time it would take the average person to complete one. I strove to be an exceptional, high-achieving student and always graduated with honors. After I tackled my schooling, equipped with my degrees, some on-the-job training, and my ambitious spirit, I set out to become the CEO of someone's company.

After receiving my master's degree, I found myself working in groups where my peers were white men and white women, with a sprinkle of an African American here or there. I was the only minority in most groups, and although that was the case, I never allowed myself to feel or act inferior. While working in a mid-level management position, I always found myself desperately seeking the approval and acceptance of a boss—who didn't look anything like me, if you know what I mean—only to be told:

You have terrible communication skills

You need more professional development

You are not ready for this kind of responsibility

A position of this magnitude is too much for you

These words became embedded in my psyche and continued to present themselves at every unsuccessful effort for promotion. I always felt sad and stuck. I felt unseen and undervalued. I just wasn't good enough. It seemed that I'd wasted both time and money going to school because all I had to show for it was an insurmountable amount of student loan debt and three pieces of paper that apparently meant nothing.

It never stopped me from trying, but that feeling of the wind being knocked out of me over and over was exhausting and kept me from being my best for a long time. I'd sunken deep into an emotional, depressive ditch. The good thing about this ditch was that there was a light I could see if I raised my head high enough. That light was my goal, and I knew that I had to reach it. I wanted to be free of feeling unworthy in an organization I was undervalued in. I realized I was responsible for my own success. Each day, I knew I had to take a step, dig my stilettos in, and climb in the direction of that success. I spent time researching my new business venture, then progressively moved forward to launch my business. I knew that to open my own organization, it would take blood, sweat, and tears. But I also knew it would be worth it because I would be doing it for myself. So I kicked the entrepreneurial door open…in my stilettos!

I want you to know your worth. I want you to be able to stand in your greatness and be non-negotiable when it comes to your wants and needs. I want you to exude confidence as you stomp on that glass ceiling, and as it cracks, you can rest assured that the shank in your stiletto is intact, because the support structure is strong and success *is* not an option, it is required.

You build that confidence during the climb. I'm not just here to help you shatter the glass ceiling. I'm here to help you navigate the glass cliff. At the end of the day, the goal for any entrepreneur—man or woman—should be to be a great businessperson and leader. If your mind is on the right track and your focus is on being the best leader you can be, you'll be on the path to climbing the cliff and through the ceiling. Here are some tips and tools that ultimately got me through my own personal journey to becoming a strong, confident woman in the workplace:

Bring Your Boldest Self to Big Challenges

Even if it doesn't come naturally to you at first, exert yourself as a bold person by readily accepting big challenges with confidence, clarity, and courage.

Challenges are a part of business, and when you lead your team through a challenge, you will shine. Try incorporating these actions into your daily routine:

- Identify priorities, develop a plan of action, and assign teams to reach the objectives without doubting yourself or second-guessing.

- Don't strive for perfection. Be self-aware, willing to take action and necessary risks, and hold yourself accountable for your mistakes. We all make them.

- Confidently communicate and be willing to hear what others have to say. Support your own decisions and be confident enough to handle any pushback.

Be Curious

Maintain a childlike curiosity when it comes to learning more about your business, the industry, and the people you hire and partner with. A healthy curiosity can be the fuel behind achieving your goals. It can be a catalyst for building relationships with your customers and team. Curiosity can replace apprehension, and it can lead to learning to negotiate more effectively, developing great products and services that fulfill your customers' needs, and formulating unique and fresh approaches to business.

Curiosity is what led me to opening my consulting agency. I was curious as to why female entrepreneurs seem to struggle in finding the tools, resources, and mentorship they need to help them transcend in business. I was curious about the ways I, as a female, and other female entrepreneurs could excel and be profitable. I wanted to find ways to help female entrepreneurs be bold, confident, and assertive and be comfortable doing it. This curiosity led me to building a tribe focused on supporting and encouraging female entrepreneurs.

Developing a healthy sense of curiosity allows you, as the CEO of your organization, to think differently. It allows you to tap into areas of your brain that aren't accessible when fear is present. Being curious isn't dangerous or irresponsible, as it is so often described. Being open-minded in this way allows you to develop more creative goals for your organization, as well as creative, unorthodox ways of achieving those goals. This can give you a competitive edge.

Think about it: As a child, some of your best attributes were likely honesty, fearlessness, inquisitiveness, resiliency, trust, and, of course, a sense of playfulness. As we get older, we lose sight of those attributes, which is common and natural, but if we infuse these qualities in our business, how can we lose? Curiosity gives us the freedom to worry less about making mistakes and more about generating favorable outcomes.

Especially as a woman, your instinct is likely to play it safe. We work so hard to climb the ladder that when we're near the top, it feels like one less-than-perfect move will send us straight back to the bottom. Trust me, the most successful men *and* women are innovators and changemakers who follow their gut and curiosity more often than you'd imagine. Give yourself permission to be curious and take your organization a step ahead of your competitors. They say curiosity killed the cat, but I think curiosity grows the business.

Networking

Networking is the meeting and forming of relationships with others both inside and outside of your industry. These relationships provide the opportunity to exchange information or services to the benefit of your respective companies. There is no argument that networking is a key factor in sustaining and growing your business.

Some benefits of networking include:

- **Learning and Collaboration Opportunities:** Networking puts you in contact with other like-minded professionals who you can learn from and partner with.

- **A Boost to Your Reputation and Brand:** Through attending social events, such as conferences, seminars, and workshops, as well as benefit gatherings and galas, you'll grow your personal profile and business reputation. Naturally, others will start to recognize your company brand as you more frequently put yourself in these positions. Your goal is for others in the industry to view you as knowledgeable, trustworthy, and supportive.

- **New Friendships:** The life of an entrepreneur can be quite lonely, especially as a woman in an industry saturated by male leaders, but through networking, you will have the opportunity to communicate with others who understand the lifestyle firsthand. These newfound friendships will expose you to new opportunities for business and personal growth, as well as provide you with the support to climb the glass cliff.

Overcoming Communication Barriers

Communication is key. This is true in practically every part of life. Communication comes in many forms and always involves at least two parties. Communication requires language and active listening. If there is a breakdown in either, problems can arise. We've all witnessed or experienced a communication barrier, where misunderstandings occurred, or tension increased due to misinterpretation.

Communication is a two-way street—always. Properly conveying information and actively listening are skills that don't come naturally for everyone, and that's okay, as long as you and the individuals on your team are willing to always be working on communication. In a workplace that encourages, respects, and honors diversity, it is crucial that everyone learns how to communicate.

We've already discussed how important it is to engage with your employees on a personal level. Easy conversation in the workplace is crucial, even when it is not work-related. This contributes to strong personal relationships.

There is certainly room for misinterpretation and disagreements in professional conversations—in meetings, for example, or among individual departments. As a leader, part of your job is keeping a level head and ensuring all of your employees are always equipped with the right information. It's also your job to ensure disagreements are defused before they cause damage to the particular department or the order of operations. Tension in the workplace can be incredibly disruptive. When it comes to moderating, be neutral, do not take sides, and, as mentioned earlier, be willing to hear everyone out.

Outside of relationships within departments and company meetings, much of the communication in the workplace is virtual. This can be isolating for some, which is why I recommend keeping communication lines open among everyone via instant messaging or chat systems. At the very least, the staff—you included—needs to be diligent when monitoring and responding to emails. As with any form of human communication, there are specific problems that can arise when communicating virtually. Be sure to implement a few rules that will alleviate common communication issues. Here are a few I think are important:

1. **Limit useless jokes, nonwork-related conversations, and unnecessary inquiries.** Granted, you want your team to get to know one another and have fun at work, but joking and personal conversations are better had during face-to-face interaction on breaks or in passing. Also, in group chats, subjecting others to personal conversations they are not

involved in only serves to distract those individuals. Furthermore, always try to figure out an answer on your own before distracting someone else with the question.

2. **Avoid the use of slang words.** Every culture has them, but they can quickly lead to confusion or frustration. Be clear—it's simple.

3. **Keep messages brief. Use concise language and avoid over-explanation.** Virtual communication is a privilege. It's quick, easy, and convenient, but this can easily be spoiled by unnecessarily long messages or emails. It seems like it would be the opposite, but the more explanation, the more of a chance for misinterpretation. Also, having a group of diverse cultures in your company brings so many benefits, but language barriers often exist as a result. Don't view this as a downfall. Instead, practice concise, clear communication. This goes hand-in-hand with the use of slang. Use basic language.

4. **Make an effort to inject a bit of personality.** One of the difficulties with virtual communication is tone. This is where the risk of misinterpretation comes in the most. In any industry, countless emails are bounced back and forth daily. While we may be animated and friendly in person, for some, it can be difficult to convey that friendliness through email, and this results in wooden, stern-sounding emails. Your main objective is getting your point across, but before pressing SEND, stop to consider how the person on the other end may feel reading your email. Take the time to inject some personality, whether that be a *"How are things going on your end?"* or a well-placed exclamation point.

Emotional Intelligence

Emotional intelligence is comprised of self-awareness, self-motivation, empathy, communication skills, and self-restraint. Emotional awareness and communication work both ways—interacting with yourself and interacting with others.

Two of my role models are Lisa Nichols and Arianna Huffington. Lisa Nichols, a motivational speaker, says, "The next time you sense a strong emotion, take some time to put your finger on exactly what you're feeling. Get quiet, turn inward, and just listen." And Arianna Huffington, author, columnist, and businesswoman, believes that "Leaders, whether you're the CEO or an individual team manager, must use emotional intelligence at work every single day. While you may not interact with every person every day, the company attitude begins with you."

Being emotionally intelligent will allow you to communicate effectively and compassionately. This starts with you looking inward and getting acquainted with your gut feelings, hopes, and dreams. Similar to curiosity, following your instinct can be crucial to your success. Be intelligent when it comes to your emotions. Take the time to evaluate them and understand them before acting on them. This can be the difference between a successful decision and a big mistake. The most important thing is to not discount your emotions, even if they are negative or ultimately not beneficial. They are still a part of you!

It is also important to be empathetic, self-aware, and in tune with those around you. In the day-to-day busyness of running an organization, it can be easy to forget your employees have emotions of their own! This is normal, and what counts is that you remind yourself to connect with those working for you and around you. Pay special attention to their responses and attitudes, and what those things might suggest about their experience working for your organization. Women are known for being more in touch with their emotions and more perceptive to others' emotions, and typically, we are seen as more approachable. While this isn't exclusively a woman's skill, take advantage of your softer, more emotional side and connect with your employees. Acknowledging emotion is not a weakness; it's a strength.

On the most basic level, have a good attitude, as Arianna Huffington suggests. Regardless of whether you chat with all your employees in person, through email, or not at all, maintaining a positive attitude will reach people in ways you don't even consider. On the days when you don't interact face to face with your employees, but you do communicate with them virtually, be sure to inject some personality into those messages, as mentioned in the section above. Positivity is contagious, and being positive can bolster your staff's happiness and engagement.

Personal Development

Personal development should be never-ending. The difference between a good leader and a great leader is the desire to push to be even better, even when you're already successful. Coaching, seminars, formal classes, or seeking a mentor or a coach are great ways to build on your existing skills and knowledge and excel. The type of personal development you pursue is largely dependent on the improvements you deem important, whether that be addressing your weaknesses or simply strengthening areas you are already satisfactory in. Just as the shank in a quality pair of stilettos can bear more weight than a cheap pair, investment in your personal growth, character, and mind sets you up to withstand even heavier challenges than you have before.

Consider if any of the sections in this book have stuck out to you thus far. If they have, that might be an area you'd benefit from focusing on. For example, maybe you need help with recruiting, networking, communication in the workplace, or business systems. Maybe you could stand to grow on a more emotional level—think confidence, charisma, public speaking, or connecting and motivating your staff and teammates.

While it's called *personal* development, this growth is important for you *and* your entire team.

SELF-CARE

Running a business and working for yourself can be just as difficult as it is rewarding. The independence of making your own decisions and reveling in your personal success is exciting. However, most entrepreneurs find it necessary to work unusual hours, endure high-pressure situations, money issues, and limited time with friends and family, which is why practicing self-care is so important.

The outsole of your stiletto is the bottom part of the shoe that comes in direct contact with the ground. In order to achieve success, you continually subject yourself to challenges, hours of hard work, and situations outside of your comfort zone. Because we're human, if we allow work to occupy too much of our lives and headspace for too long without self-care, we allow our tough, slip-resistant exterior to wear down. When that happens, we are liable to slip and crumble, just as a pair of timeworn, unmaintained heels aren't safe on a slick tile floor. In order to be a successful female in the workplace and have the fortitude to face challenges head-on, you need to maintain your body, mind, and personal life and happiness.

In our society, it's commonplace to do for others and put everyone else before ourselves, but taking time for you is an absolute must. Self-care is not selfish; rather, it will keep you focused, energized, and productive. While the term *self-care* often draws up images of bubble baths or binge-watching TV, in a more basic sense, it simply means taking time for what you want to do. This can include setting aside time to grow as a businessperson outside of your actual work responsibilities.

Today, we go, go, go, without taking the time to connect with our goals and dreams. Self-care is about freeing up that mental space once in a while for whatever you'd like to fill it with. That might be a class, exercise, business planning, meditation, or shoe shopping. Whatever you choose, that take is pivotal for your mental health and ultimate success.

Money Matters

Set aside time to address your personal financial goals. Creating and maintaining a personal budget will provide you with a clear picture of your income versus expenses. You should never commingle your business finances with your personal finances. Your personal budget will prevent overspending or failing to pay bills in a timely manner, and it will also allow you to set aside funds to support your hobbies, socializing, and self-care. Being financially stable is the first step toward a healthy work-life balance. With this foundation in place, you'll be able to take time for yourself without that lingering guilt so many of us are familiar with.

When it comes to budgeting, here is some valuable advice:

Step 1. Prioritize Where Your Money Goes

What's the most important thing you spend money on each month? Groceries? Rent? Fast food? Your gym membership? Socializing? If you work for yourself, is it office expenses? Is it payroll?

In order to organize a viable financial plan, you need to first evaluate what you spend money on and where those expenses fall as a priority. Obviously, in a dire financial situation, you would want to continue allocating as much money as possible to the things at the top of the list, like your rent or mortgage, food, and payroll for your employees, while forgetting things at the bottom of your list, like entertainment or social events.

This may seem like a simple or skippable part of the process, but it's actually critical to designing a budget that will work for you. If you have any kind of debt, you should put that at the top of the list. Organize it by interest rate, with the highest interest rates being of higher priority, because you want to pay them down sooner. Your money priorities should also align with your personal values. That means the largest segments of your budget should reflect what you consider most important, whether that be business growth or personal care.

Once you have organized your biggest priorities, you can then see where you can cut back in order to maximize your ability to invest in your true priorities. Of course, your priorities will change over time, so you should make plans to come back and re-evaluate your financial priorities as you pay down debts and find your personal values shifting.

Step 2. Estimate Your Anticipated Income

If you're working for yourself, you may not be working on a steady salary, but it's still important to estimate your monthly income. Failing to do so will lead to money mishaps. After all, you've surely heard the saying, "What gets measured gets managed." Not knowing how much you bring in every month (at least on average) will lead to poor money management, which could get you into trouble.

Your estimated monthly income may raise and lower over time, and because of that, it's safer to underestimate than overestimate. Decide how you will divvy up the minimum amount you expect to earn each month across your biggest financial priorities, and then decide how any additional income will be divided among all the things you have identified as financial priorities, working your way down the list.

Step 3. Understand Your Expenses

Most of us have some level of discretionary spending, even if we don't budget for it. It could be those impulse buys at the cash register, which get lost in our general food budget, or it could be something more obvious, like new clothes, subscriptions, or trips. In any case, it's important that you understand where your money is going, down to the dollar. This will really help you analyze how much you are devoting to your biggest financial priorities and, more importantly, show you how much you're spending on things that may not be so important to you.

Work backward, analyzing your spending for the past three to twelve months to see where all of your money has gone. This means bringing out your credit card and bank statements, along with any records of checks, withdrawals, and any bills you have paid. Add everything up, and you'll see how much you've spent in each category. Going forward, certain financial apps or software can be used to budget and automatically categorize your expenses for a quick snapshot of your ongoing spending and how it changes over time.

Step 4. Make a Plan for Saving

Everyone should be saving some amount of money, even if you don't have a big purchase or expense planned. You may be saving for retirement, a rainy day, or something specific, like paying off your car, buying a home, or going on a big trip. If you have a specific goal, you'll be able to work toward a specific number. However, even if you do not have a specific goal in sight, you should be allocating a good chunk of your income to savings.

There are resources available to aid in your savings journey, as well as successful women who can serve as role models for you as you learn about money management, such as Mary Callahan Erdoes, who is the CEO of J.P. Morgan, and Abigail Johnson, CEO of Fidelity

Investments. There are also many influencers who can provide you with sound and solid advice as it pertains to money, such as Patrice Washington, author of *Real Money Answers for Every Woman,* Samantha Ealy, Founder and CEO of Generation Wealthy, and Tarra Jackson a.k.a. Madam Money.

If you prefer to use apps, there is an abundance of apps available, like Mint for all things finance, Personal Capital for wealth management, Clarity Money, which is great for managing subscriptions, and Prism for bill payment.

When it comes to finding money to save, you again need to look back on your spending habits and see how they stack up against your financial priorities. Look to cut down—or cut out completely—any spending that falls into your low-priority categories. You should also look into some creative money-saving tactics—a common one is cooking more of your own food rather than eating out. Simple changes like this are great for your wallet and can help you on your path toward other goals, like financial security, which leads to better self-care and wellness.

Step 5. Stick to Your Plan

The key to a successful plan is sticking to it, which is why you need to be fully committed to whatever financial plan you come up with. In order to ensure your success, you need to make sure, at the time of planning, that your financial plan is realistic and achievable. You also need to clearly define any financial changes you need to make, like how much you need to cut down on spending overall in order to achieve your savings goals.

As with any plan, you'll need to re-evaluate and refine over time. Do this often. I suggest sitting down once a month to review all of your financials. This gives you the opportunity to make sure that you are on track with your goals and that you are living up to the plan you have designed for yourself. This regular check-in will keep you consistent and on track.

Step 6. Expect the Unexpected

Did you know that an unexpected financial expense of just $400 could push more than one-third of Americans into a difficult financial situation? The key to being financially stable is to expect the unexpected. This means being smart with your money and, as mentioned, building up an emergency fund or rainy-day account.

Having accessible liquid funds is key, no matter what your income or long-term financial goals are. You simply never know what might happen, and having money to deal with unexpected problems, whether it's paying your insurance deductible or covering any number of circumstances, will be key to keeping you on track during a hardship. Stashing away just a hundred dollars per month could save you a lot of headaches down the road.

Personal Growth

You never want to become stagnant, but unfortunately, many people eventually do. Active personal growth is the key to continuously moving forward in every aspect of your life, and being able to understand and develop yourself is essential to achieving your full potential. Working on your personal development each and every day will help you grow, mature, and continuously fulfill your goals in both your career and personal life.

Fortunately, more and more people are beginning to shift their focus toward self-improvement (that's surely one of the reasons you're reading this book). It needs to be a more conscious part of our routines. You should also make sure that your self-improvement isn't purely focused on acquiring new material things or improving superficial aspects of your life and self. If that's where your focus is, you're searching in the wrong places. Your personal growth needs to start from within.

As an entrepreneur, I have been able to enjoy a steady increase in my income, resulting in a salary of over six figures. I've experienced vacations in places I never thought I would visit, and I've purchased my dream car. But all of these wonderful things have come from a long, sometimes hard, road of being an entrepreneur.

It's safe to say I have a solid understanding of professional growth, which I've been developing throughout my career. But personal growth is different and a more recent journey of mine. I was excited to participate in a seven-day personal development retreat in the Bahamas. It was through this journey of personal discovery that I was able to grow and expand my thinking, heal past traumas, and emerge as a refreshed and stronger person.

Once you begin working on your personal growth and facing and conquering challenges, you will find that you are naturally more motivated and more confident. You will be inspired to learn and grow, and you'll also be more excited about potential opportunities—and more apt to find them. Growing on a personal level will help you expand your world, making you more aware of the possibilities and people that are all around you.

The great news is that it's not that hard to work on your personal growth. In fact, it really starts with the smallest changes in your day-to-day life. Try these tips to begin working on your personal growth:

- **Look to learn new things.** Learning about other cultures, people, and ways of life will help expand your mind while building a useful knowledge base. You'll see yourself looking at the world differently, and you'll build empathy in the process. You can learn by reading, watching documentaries, or, better yet, getting out there and doing things yourself.

- **Travel often.** Even if you can't travel to some faraway place, getting out and interacting with your own community is a great start. Simply traveling to neighboring cities and states will introduce you to all sorts of new experiences while building character in the process.

- **Be kind to others.** Connecting with those around you is imperative to being a well-rounded person, and there is no better way to begin interacting with those around you than simply being kind to them. You'll notice a shift in your own mindset and a huge increase in your own positivity when you are kind to others, whether it's volunteering in your free time or simply holding the door for someone next time you go out.

- **Organize your space.** It can be very difficult for most people to focus when they are disorganized. Even if you do not feel that disorganization or clutter is affecting you, taking the time to organize your home and workspace can drastically improve your mental health and productivity. When your physical surroundings are in order, you will find it easier to get your thoughts and ideas in order as well.

- **Put things into perspective.** Making snap judgments is human nature, but this can also be detrimental to our points of view. When judging someone's actions or a particular situation, always try to imagine at least three potential reasons or scenarios. It's too easy to get caught up in one mode of thinking. Being able to see every side of a story and understand another person's point of view is a big sign of personal growth, so get into the habit of doing this. A diverse way of thinking can also help you through tough challenges.

All of these methods will help fuel personal growth. Seek to work some of them into your routine on a daily basis.

Self-esteem

When you take care of yourself, you nourish your self-esteem and self-worth. Undoubtedly, professional success in your career can definitely boost self-esteem, but simply taking pride in yourself as an individual will enhance it as well.

When it comes to building self-esteem, the most important thing is refraining from self-criticism or negative self-talk. When you feel that familiar doubt creep in, you must battle those thoughts with gratitude and pride. We all have doubts, but we also all have accomplishments and unique attributes that should be celebrated.

Acceptance is ultimately something that everyone seeks. First, you must look within. It's impossible to feel comfortable in your own skin if you don't accept yourself, inside and out. You are unique! You have something valuable to contribute! You are enough! Believing these things is easier said than done, and it takes practice, but the practice is worthwhile.

Acceptance is a fundamental need, and while others' opinions of you should not be a priority, you can fulfill this need in a healthy way by surrounding yourself with positive, like-minded individuals. Working with others with similar goals and interests, and being an integral part of a particular group or tribe, is a great way to feel fulfilled and accepted while staying true to yourself.

Taking care of yourself will also help you feel more confident. It's common to find a newfound sense of confidence when working on a personal goal. To ensure success, that goal should be connected to some of your deepest passions, whether that is health and wellness, being a better cook, reading X number of books a year, or achieving a promotion at work. If you commit to a plan—for example, working out four days a week or reading two books a month—you'll likely feel your self-esteem improving simply from sticking to the plan and accomplishing your day-to-day goals.

It's important to learn to lift yourself up, because the reality is, you are the only one who will always be with you, no matter what. Outside of the workplace or strict self-improvement goals, consider learning a new skill, exploring a hobby you've put on the back burner, helping someone in need, or doing something creative. Spending time on what you want to do rather than what you feel others want you to do or what you need to do is a way to nurture yourself. Also, learning new skills, helping others, or creating something beautiful is something to be proud of, and pride in yourself—in healthy doses—is good for you!

Finding ways to invest in yourself generates self-respect. Self-respect links to your sense of integrity in both your personal and professional life, and when you are equipped with this, along with high self-esteem, you will be able to navigate the world without crippling self-doubt and anxiety. In the long run, you'll go farther and achieve more.

Mindset

Self-care, in actuality, is a mindset. When you acknowledge what you need in order to be happy and fulfilled and go after it, you are taking full responsibility for your own well-being and happiness. This is empowering. It also oftentimes takes the pressure off others who may feel responsible for you, and it will, in turn, transform the time you spend with friends and family. Gathering together should be about enjoying each other's company, rather than being built on unrealistic expectations.

In October 2019, I attended a Lisa Nichols Dynamic Women Retreat. It was the first time I remember truly investing in my personal development. My entire life had been focused on *professional* development. It was at this retreat that I was able to upgrade my mindset. For the first time in my life, I was able to identify my limiting beliefs, my hurdles, and my self-esteem issues, face them, and walk away with a refreshed vision for my life and my business. I was able to reprogram my brain for positivity, empowerment, and success. This, for me, was life-changing. I found out how to best take care of myself and, as a result, be my best self when serving others. In other words, I learned to put my oxygen mask on first before running to help others.

Below, I've included some tips I've picked up along the way, from retreats, like I mentioned, and also from just *living*. I encourage you to check, change, and improve your mindset.

Take Note of Your Self-Talk

Ever heard someone trying to hype themselves up before a big moment or event? There's actual science behind this tactic. Outside of scenarios like this, your self-talk usually isn't spoken aloud. Self-talk happens in our minds as we go about our daily business, and it's important that you tune in to the things you're telling yourself. Make a habit out of regularly evaluating your self-talk and correcting yourself when it's negative.

No one is safe. I've been a victim of my own self-talk: I was ugly and fat. Nobody liked me. I was unlovable. I was unwanted. I would never be successful. My business would fail. Nobody would ever want to work for me.

Some of this, or maybe all of it, probably sounds familiar to you.

This negativity was running through my mind, both consciously and unconsciously, all the time. Over time, I've been able to fight this negative self-talk by finding ways to drown it out. My secret weapon is daily affirmations. They are Post-it Notes everywhere: in my home, in my office, and even in daily notifications I receive on my phone.

When you find yourself speaking negatively about your own appearance, capabilities, or likelihood of success, change that doubt into empowerment. It doesn't seem like much, but simply thinking to yourself, "I can do this," will make a huge difference in your mindset, and when you nurture your mindset, there will be a domino effect. How you think affects how you feel, and ultimately how you act and how you show up in the world.

Change How You Speak

It isn't just the voice inside your head that matters. Once you have taken note of how you think to yourself and about yourself, you should begin being more mindful of how you speak to others. A negative mindset is difficult to keep to yourself.

We've all known a chronic complainer, right? That person who can talk for hours on end about all the short sticks they've drawn. There was a lady like this who worked for me. Her name was Debbie. I called her Debbie Downer. I never wanted to engage in conversation with her. It's hard to walk away from that type of person feeling light and happy. One person's negativity has a way of spreading and bringing others down. The truth is, these people are often doing so without even realizing it. That's why it is so important to keep your thoughts in check and also what you share aloud in check. You don't want to be Debbie. If you find you have only negative things to discuss, keep them to yourself, and first trace those topics back to the root.

Conquer your negativity instead of spreading it. This all goes back to mindset. Next time you have a conversation with someone, make an effort to talk about something positive rather than complaining or pointing out the negatives of a situation. This will encourage a mindset that focuses on abundance and success.

Define Your Ideal Mindset

Everyone has different goals and plans, which means not everyone will benefit from the exact same mindset. We all have different values and priorities. Some value stability and contentment, while others seek continuous advancement. This goes for work, physical fitness, education, etc. In general, it would be ideal for us all to have an optimistic, positive foundation on which to build our goals.

Your mindset is likely to shift a bit depending on whether you have specific goals you are currently working toward. For example, when it comes to striving for professional success, there is plenty of talk about how "successful" people think. There are books, articles, and podcasts delving into reframing your mindset, specifically to achieve success. These are all great resources for learning about how successful people think. Learning about the power of mindset and how the brain works, in general, is becoming a hot topic for individuals looking to maximize their potential, no matter their definition of "success."

Look for Like-Minded People

Surrounding yourself with like-minded people is the way to go. If you want to be healthier, you need to hang out with people who care about nourishing their bodies. If you want to earn more money, you need to hang out with people who are business focused and driven. Above all, you need to avoid hanging out with people who contradict whatever goals you are working toward, as they will only hold you back and bring you down.

As an entrepreneur, this can be difficult. Oftentimes, we find ourselves not having time for networking or other social activities. I am familiar with having more tasks to complete than there are hours in the day. We tend to bury ourselves in work 24/7, but we forget to remind ourselves that the work is never actually finished. Has there ever been a time when you took multitasking to the extent of insanity instead of getting out of your own head, getting out of the office, and attending social activities that allow you to unwind and just breathe? My answer is yes, and I'm going to guess that your answer is yes also.

I'm giving you permission to step away from your desk, step away from your office, step away from your piles of paperwork and company obligations and seek out those like-minded individuals who understand what you're going through and can help you re-evaluate and get your mindset back on a positive track.

Build Habits That Support the Right Mindset

You cannot change your mindset unless you put that change into action. Change your day-to-day habits in order to support your new mindset. Reinforcing your new thinking with refined action will ensure you experience the results of a better mindset.

For example, maybe you're interested in being a more positive employee and want to start feeling better at work. You could set an earlier alarm rather than sleeping until the last minute, take a refreshing shower, and use the extra time to look your best and feel great before stepping into work.

Since the Dynamic Women Retreat, I've made it my daily responsibility to connect to my tribe regularly in order to stay motivated. I also enjoy yoga and practice daily manifestation techniques, including visualizations and affirmations.

I suggest setting aside some time to journal about your daily life. This can help tremendously, as it will give you time to reflect on your accomplishments and what you learn with each passing day. Plus, there is something concrete about putting things in writing that makes tackling small and large goals even more satisfying.

Me Time

Taking time for yourself allows you to rejuvenate. You might consider "me time" as enjoying a cup of coffee or tea while reading a good book, taking a walk out in nature, attending a yoga class, or escaping to a quiet space for meditation. Below are a few other ideas for quality "me time."

- **Challenge Yourself.** Want to build character? You can work on your personal growth during your "me time" by finding a way to break out of your comfort zone or otherwise challenge yourself on a personal level. This could mean engaging in a public social event if you are quite shy, or it could be spending some time in a brand-new, unfamiliar place. Activities that are outside of your usual day-to-day plan can offer new knowledge and fun times—think about taking a surfing lesson or heading out for a cooking class.

- **Get Creative.** Spending time doing something that activates the creative regions of your brain can benefit you long after "me time" is over. This could be as simple as sitting down with a de-stressing adult coloring book, or you could pick up a new instrument or experiment with a new craft. Whatever you choose to do, focus not on how good you are, but rather on how creative you can be. Think outside the box.

- **Expand Your Horizons.** If you love being out and about, maybe you'd love to spend some "me time" at a museum, an art gallery, or another exhibit where you can take the time to relax and be cultured at the same time. You could also venture outside if you love nature. Go for a hike or perhaps try a low-key hobby like geocaching, which allows you to explore all new places while hunting for hidden surprises.

- **Update Your Look.** A classic way to spend some "me time" every once in a while is to update your look. If you find that your hair, makeup, or fashion choices fall by the wayside when you're busy, maybe you'd enjoy spending some of your "me time" refreshing an element of your appearance. Get creative with a new makeup look or opt for a different haircut than usual. Buy new stilettos. Taking the time to focus on yourself is a great way to decompress, and it can also do wonders to boost your self-esteem.

- **Take a class.** Who says you can't be productive during "me time?" Taking a class is a great way to spend your free time. This can help you with your personal development goals, and the skills you learn could even help you in your professional life at some point. The main priority, though, is that you take a class for something that you enjoy or have always been interested in, be it painting, cooking, photography, or something else entirely. Alternatively, you could volunteer or join a mentorship program so that you could help others learn new skills.

- **Exercise your brain.** Something as simple as a sudoku puzzle can exercise your brain and keep you sharp, which is why it's a favorite pastime for many people. There are also plenty of apps you can download that have brain puzzles you can do to pass the time and improve your mental acuity.

Whatever "me time" is for you, put it on your schedule and honor yourself by doing it.

PROFESSIONALISM

You're reading this book because you are a professional CEO. Where you are in your career differs from other readers, but we all have one thing in common—we want to be the best we can be and achieve the success that reflects that.

We've talked about your role as a leader when it comes to establishing a positive company culture and employee experience, implementing effective business systems, navigating the business world, especially as a woman, and then on a basic level, caring for yourself and your mental health during your quest for success. These are imperative to building a successful organization and building a successful you by developing your leadership skills and maintaining your mental health. The cherry on top is how you present to the world the person you've become.

On the surface, stilettos accentuate the leg. This look is widely accepted as aesthetically pleasing. On top of an attractive, put-together appearance, many of us can attest to feeling more confident in a pair of heels, whether it be the height, the strut that accompanies them, or the overall outfit they complement. What sets a pair of stilettos apart from other types of shoes is the high heel, and what sets you apart from your competitors is your professionalism. You can have the most knowledge, have seen the highest levels of success, or possess the best business strategies, but what matters is how you present those attributes and show them to the world, through your day-to-day interactions. The truth is, appearances do matter.

Furthermore, the more pride you take in all points of your professionalism, the stronger professional you'll be, which in turn attracts new relationships, opportunities, and credibility. Just like a high-quality heel can bear more weight, a strong sense of professionalism can carry you through the business world.

Professionalism is about making the right impression and maintaining your personal and brand integrity, as well as being well received by others, which leads to comfortable, meaningful connections and employees who want to work for *you*.

Here's a look at the pillars of professionalism:

Confidence

Striving to be more confident? You're not alone. Lack of confidence is a major problem affecting an average of 78% of women who say they don't feel completely confident in their appearance. Even more women struggle to be confident in themselves overall. It goes without saying that this is an issue for those who want to be in leadership positions. A lack of confidence could be the one thing that holds you back.

Psychological studies have shown that people feel more confident during times of stress—like at public speaking engagements—if they stand in a "power pose," with their hands on their hips. This proves that good posture is one way to look and feel more confident and professional overall, but simply standing up straight isn't enough for many women who struggle with self-esteem.

We all want to be that well-dressed woman in heels, smiling, making eye contact, and acknowledging others. We all want to be that commanding presence. Confidence is all about how you feel and how you present yourself to the world as a result, but other accessories can offer an assist, such as your smile, a firm handshake, and eye contact. Even if you're not the most confident person in the room yet, mimic the behaviors of the woman you envision and want to be. While "fake it till you make it" doesn't apply in all areas, it does in this one!

I was invited to a networking event for women, which was showcasing a twelve-month leadership program that attendees could enroll in. I am, by nature, an introvert. I'm not normally comfortable in groups of strangers. I had anxiety the entire day leading up to the event, but I decided to go. I was, after all, overly committed to developing my leadership skills.

Still, while looking for a parking space, I contemplated not going in. I found a hundred excuses to leave, but I forced myself to park and checked my makeup in the mirror. Then I walked into the restaurant where the meeting was being held. I had purposely arrived late, thinking I would miss the networking session and just show up for the presentation. I arrived approximately ten minutes before the presentation was to start, which was perfect.

I scanned the room, finding that everyone was already in conversation with others. I had a few options: walk up to an already formed group, stand there and wait for someone to approach me, or sit down and pretend to check emails. Before I had time to decide, a lady smiled in my direction, excitedly said, "Hi!" and began to walk my way. I exhaled, smiled, and said, "Hi," happy she was moving in my direction. As she approached, I realized I had no idea who she was. She reached out her hand for a handshake, and just as I reached out, she walked right past me and started talking to another woman behind me.

I just stood there, paralyzed with embarrassment, until the meeting started. I was humiliated, and clearly, the memory has stuck with me, even though that woman probably didn't think twice about it, even in the moment. But that was a long time ago. Now, before I walk into a crowded room, I take a couple of deep breaths. Then, as soon as I walk in, I start talking. I'll walk up to an individual or a group of people without hesitancy and immediately introduce myself. My confidence has improved because it had to. It's not easy being an introvert when networking is a major part of your job, but it's not impossible either. Many shy individuals are successful businesspeople. It just takes a bit of extra effort. You wouldn't know it, but Audrey Hepburn, Christina Aguilera, Rosa Parks, and Lady Gaga are all successful female introverts.

Just remind yourself why networking is important. As entrepreneurs, we need to know who is in the room and how we can benefit from connecting with them. I can now be deliberate in making important connections that benefit my business and my brand. I can set aside my insecurities to fuel my success, and I can do this because I've built confidence in my knowledge, capability, and overall self-worth.

Networking is just one aspect that can improve from a healthy dose of confidence. Improving your confidence also helps if you struggle with public speaking, negotiating, attracting customers, or human relations. Aside from your stilettos, confidence is one of the most important things to wear.

Communication

Unfortunately, there is still a divide between women and men in the workplace, and in some areas, women must work harder. Communication is one of them. As a woman, your communication needs to be impeccable. It needs to be persuasive without being pushy. It needs to be intentional without coming across as tough or aggressive. While no two women are exactly alike, and we all have different styles of communication and different personalities, just like men do, women need to be more careful to articulate well in order to not be blocked from being heard, valued, respected, or appreciated.

Scientifically, women's and men's brains are just different. According to Dr. Louann Brizendine:

In the centers for language and hearing, for example, women have 11% more neurons than men. The principal hub of both emotion and memory formation—the hippocampus—is also larger in the female brain, as is the brain circuitry for language and observing emotions in others. The female brain has tremendous unique aptitudes— outstanding verbal agility, the ability to connect deeply in friendship, a nearly psychic capacity to read faces and tone of voice for emotions and states of mind, and the ability to defuse conflict. All of this is hardwired into the brains of women. These are the talents women are born with that many men, frankly, are not.

While it's common for women to be discounted in the workplace, keep these things in mind. We actually have the superpower of being great communicators!

There were times in the past when communication was specified as a reason that I did not deserve to be promoted. While I never particularly agreed with my superiors' decisions, it was clear that I needed to find ways to communicate more effectively in the workplace. This didn't mean that I was a *bad* communicator, but that I needed to mold my style of communication to suit the environment.

Fortunately for me, improving my communication skills helped launch me into the entrepreneurial arena and assisted me in attaining the success that I have today. Here are some things I learned along the way:

- Communication has three aspects: your words, your tone, and your body language.

- Words are not always the most important of the three. More than 50% of communication is nonverbal clues.

- Learn what your nonverbal clues are saying and how to read them in others. I had to master active listening. Most people do not practice this. It means to digest the entire conversation—both what is being said and what is not being said. I learned to communicate with power and finesse in a way that makes others comfortable, and by *others*, I mean men. This is mostly due to picking up on nonverbal clues and directing the conversation accordingly. When you become accustomed to tuning in to someone else's body language, facial expression, and tone, it becomes easier to interpret how they are receiving you.

- Also, have other things to talk about other than work. Read the newspaper, watch the news, learn some fun facts to bring up during conversations. This is key to bonding with others and making them feel at ease in your presence.

- Lastly, learn to code switch. The way to speak with your girlfriends over drinks is not the way to communicate during an important negotiation meeting.

Working on good communication is a great way to boost your confidence. When you're confident in your communication skills, you'll feel comfortable going into any situation. For more practice, consider hiring a coach, joining a class, or taking an online course to help you practice better verbal and written communication skills.

Positive Attitude

You've probably heard people say that it's "all in the attitude," and they were completely right. Your attitude affects how you feel, how you make others feel, and how you react in different situations.

Professionalism requires a positive attitude—not an overly optimistic or unrealistic one, but one that enables you to see roadblocks and hurdles as opportunities to do something different and better. Working on a positive attitude is easier for some people than others, but the key is to focus on changing your mindset on a day-to-day basis, as we covered in the previous chapter. If you commit to a mindset makeover, you'll see your overall perspective shifting with time.

Ethics

Having strong ethics is such a fundamental part of being a successful professional and a happy human being. Without them, people often find themselves aimlessly chasing profit and losing all meaning in the midst of difficult career goals and personal setbacks.

Fortunately, you probably already have a set of strong ethics. Now, you just need to remind yourself to stick by them no matter what. You may find that it helps to write these ethics out and explain why each one is so important to you.

Integrity

The ability to stand by your ethics even in the most trying of situations is called integrity, and it's another pillar of professionalism. Someone who is willing to toss their ethics aside for the promise of a big paycheck or easier solution doesn't have integrity.

While money and dubious business deals can certainly tempt even the strongest of women, taking that road is never the right choice. Stay true to your integrity, even if it means taking the more difficult path.

Honesty goes hand in hand with integrity. Being an honest person of integrity will earn the trust of those around you, and that's not something money can buy.

Humility

There's no doubt that you should be proud of your accomplishments, and you should certainly let those around you know about the great things you have achieved. However, you have to be tactful when sharing about your accomplishments, or it will easily come across as bragging—and, at some point, it can begin to turn into bragging.

Humility is a tricky but important skill to practice because, without it, you'll find yourself alienating those around you and be perceived as self-absorbed or egotistical. Talk to people about your achievements when relevant, but don't bring them up all the time.

Let your success speak for itself.

Reliability

People want to know that they can count on you to get the job done. Reliability is all about follow-through, attention to detail, and commitment to finishing what you start.

You can consider yourself reliable if you always do your best to fulfill promises and avoid making promises you can't keep. Life happens, but you should always seek to uphold expectations, meet deadlines, and communicate when things don't go according to the original plan.

Consistency

Like integrity and honesty, consistency and reliability go hand in hand. When someone considers you reliable, it means they are counting on you to consistently offer the same great level of service to clients, even when you're having a bad day. It also means consistently showing up for employees and delivering on your responsibilities.

It's important to clients and employees that you are consistent. It leaves them no room to second-guess choosing you to serve them or choosing you to lead them, and it leaves them little room to wonder if you'll deliver.

Appearance

Appearance is an important part of everyone's professional image, and although the look of a "professional" may vary from industry to industry, with some requiring traditional formal attire and others enabling you to be a bit more expressive, it's important that you're always presentable.

This means considering your hair, nails, and wardrobe. Taking pride in your appearance leads to others receiving you well, not just because you look good, but because it's clear that you value yourself. This ties back in with good self-care and confidence, so while appearance is last on this list, it certainly shouldn't be last on yours!

The Final Touch

As you prepare to take on the day, the last touch is slipping into your stilettos, which will support you and hold you up as you create an outstanding organization and become a fearless leader. They have been crafted for professional women like you, from the counter, which maintains the structure of the shoe, the tip, which fits your toes perfectly while allowing a bit of room to grow, the collar that shapes the shoe and holds your foot in place, to the shank that supports your arch and bears your weight, the outsole, which provides traction and protects you from the harsh concrete, and finally, the heel, which adds a bit of flair, amplifies your appearance, and holds you upright and tall.

Just as the counter, tip, collar, shank, outsole, and heel come together to shape a shoe you can be comfortable in while navigating the business world—as long as they've been manufactured and assembled with care—the pivotal points discussed in this book can shape a successful organization and career if you execute them well and with confidence and clear judgment.

A strong, healthy workplace culture is the foundation of any organization, and within that culture, a positive employee experience will bloom. Utilizing key business systems will ensure that the organization's operations are strong and complement the workplace culture you've created.

Every business leader experiences hurdles along the way, and it's no secret that women have a higher chance of experiencing more than average. Maintaining focus on being the best leader you can be while navigating the glass cliff is essential to overcoming these obstacles. Furthermore, the business world, while exciting and rewarding, can be draining and overwhelming. Practicing self-care will keep you afloat. It's important to keep your head on straight, and that's impossible to do without taking time for yourself.

All of these aspects come together to shape a successful organization and leader. Once you build this foundation, all that's left to do is get dressed, put on a smile, strap on your stilettos, and walk into your destiny.

REFERENCES

1. https://www.ziprecruiter.com/blog/how-to-recognize-outstanding-employee-performance/

2. https://www.inc.com/melanie-curtin/employees-who-feel-heard-are-46x-more-likely-to-feel-empowered-to-do-their-best-work.html

3. https://www2.deloitte.com/us/en/pages/human-capital/topics/bersin-insights-and-services-for-hr.html

4. https://blog.grabcad.com/blog/2019/02/05/4-reasons-why-companies-need-to-be-investing-in-tech-in-2019/

5. https://www.gallup.com/workplace/236375/engaged-remote-workforce.aspx

6. https://www.cnbc.com/2019/05/23/millions-of-americans-are-only-400-away-from-financial-hardship.html

7. https://www.salesforce.com/blog/2017/07/impact-of-equality-business-research.html?d=7010M000001yv8PQAQ)

8. https://everyonesocial.com/blog/employee-engagement-statistics/

9. https://www.developgoodhabits.com/fixed-mindset-vs-growth-mindset/

10. https://www.daveramsey.com/blog/the-truth-about-budgeting

11. https://www.forbes.com/sites/payout/2017/09/19/practicing-self-care-is-important-10-easy-habits-to-get-you-started/#33111f27283a

12. https://www.forbes.com/sites/sarazervos/2016/08/02/12-career-business-tips-from-successful-women/

13. https://www.inc.com/peter-gasca/10-great-tips-to-empower-female-entrepreneurs.html

14. Forbes.com
https://www.forbes.com/sites/kathycaprino/2012/12/06/the-top-6-communication-challenges-professional-women-face/#2e4b1e5f4f00

Let's Stay Connected

  https://www.instagram.com/garri_davis/

  https://www.facebook.com/LeadHerCeo/

Website: www.garridavisagency.com

Email: garridavis@icloud.com

Phone: 513-375-1267

This book was published with the support of The Bestsellers Academy.

Do you have a book on the inside of you?

Let us get your story out of your belly and into an international bestselling book!

Phone: 1-868-374-7441

Email: success@thebestsellersacademy.com

Website: TheBestsellersAcademy.com

www.ingramcontent.com/pod-product-compliance
Lightning Source LLC
Chambersburg PA
CBHW031950190326
41519CB00007B/743